BLUE MOON

literary & art review

Novel Excerpts – Short Stories – Poems
Paintings – Photographs – Reviews

Issue 20

Blue Moon Literary & Art Review

Founder: Scott Evans

Editor: Scott Evans
Proofreader: Cynthia Cooper Evans
Poetry Editor: Gayle Jansen Beede
Assistant Editor: Adam Russ
Layout Designer: Josh Tulman

Front Cover: Ian Walkley
Back Cover: Ian Walkley

Publisher:
Blue Moon Literary & Art Publishing
327 Twelfth St., Davis, CA 95616
www.bluemoonlitartreview.com
530.902.0026
Email: evans327@comcast.net

Short Stories, Excerpts, & Poems

Cover Artist: Ian Walkley

Born in Tasmania and now based in Brisbane, Australia, Ian Walkley has more than twenty years as a marketing professional, including working in government and establishing a successful market research consultancy. After selling his business in 2008, Ian pursued writing and published his first novel No Remorse *in 2012, at a time when ebooks had thrown the publishing industry into a disruptive depression.* No Remorse *won an international thriller award, but Ian moved into selling real estate for an income, keeping writing and painting as aspirational sidelines. Ian is now retired and continues to write novels and paint. He enjoys both realism and abstract forms including fluid acrylics. His favorite artist is Kandinsky and he loves the palette knife works of Leonid Afremov. His novel* No Remorse *is available on Amazon with 4.3 stars, and is highly relevant with current events in the world.*

BLUE MOON

The Best Days
by Paige E. Reecer

Before the smoking, the drinking, the sporadic use of drugs, the constant bad taste in men, my mother was beautiful.

Not in a conventional way. No, she had thin lips, hooded eyes, thin hair that never knew if it wanted to be wavy or straight, and a waif frame. But she had a beauty to her that was electric, magnetic and when I look at photographs of her, I study the planes of her face, the contours of her jaw, the softness of her brow, unable to look away until I start noticing the parts of her that are me.

Then I flip the photograph over.

* * *

I sifted through the clothes at the thrift store, looking for something funky, something bright, loud, fun. Coming to the thrift store is a Sunday ritual for my husband and me. Some people go to church, we go thrifting. It works for us. My husband sighed, ready to go look at the books and equipment tucked away at the back of the store. I asked him to give me five more minutes and he made me pinky promise. We never break our pinky promises.

Feeling generous, I cut my time looking through the clothes and headed toward the back. Before we made it, my husband stopped and turned around.

"We need to go. Now."

He knew I hated making small talk with extended family or people we went to high school with just a few years ago, so leaving places early or going the long way around to avoid being seen was common, but the look in his eyes and the strain in his voice concerned me.

"Why? Who is it?"

"Please, let's just go."

I peered over his shoulder. In a snug pair of jeans and flowy top stood my mother, looking at a row of coffee cups.

* * *

My mother had me at a young age, some time in her early twenties in 1966, and her figure bounced back rather quickly from childbirth. It was something she prided herself on, going back to her pre-baby body so soon. She never let me forget the stretch marks, though, or the purple scar from the C-section. In all those old pictures in the months after my birth, my mother always had her hair dyed and curled, paired with a slash of red lipstick and fitted blouse. And she made sure I was in frilly little dresses with shiny Mary Janes over my bobby socks. Perched on a cocked hip, I looked like a wild mess of ribbon and tulle. She looked like one of those movie stars that carries their little dogs with them everywhere.

We were the best of friends, she'd tell me.

"You were my little buddy, Pumpkin. I'd strap you in the car seat, roll the windows down, and we'd cruise for miles. Just you and me and the open road."

Where my mother was beautiful, I was ugly. I had a big, bald, round head that didn't sprout curls until I was a year and a half and I was so chunky, my feet hardly fit into my church shoes and when they did, little mounds of fat would puff out over the straps. But oh, did my mother think I was the darlingest thing.

"Your little pumpkin-head was so stinkin' cute and you had the sweetest smile. Oh stop it, you weren't ugly. I don't make ugly kids."

As a baby, I was a nomad. I slept in more pulled-out dressers and pallets on the floor than I did my crib. A village of people helped raise me before my mother met Paul. My Nana, my Uncle Travis's girlfriend Jess, my mother's friend Tina, and my Aunt Lacey all stepped in to help my mother while she worked late nights and early mornings to put food on the table and dresses on my back.

My Aunt Jess looked over at me one day after I got home from school, dish towel thrown over her shoulder, hands scrubbing the dishes in soapy water.

"You know your mother would just leave you with me for a whole weekend, not tell anyone, not your Nana, not your Uncle Travis. No one. She just up and left and left me and your uncle to make sure you stayed alive. You won't believe how many classes I had to take you to while I was in college. I was only eighteen too and your uncle and I had only been dating but just a few months. Oh yeah, I'd have to lug you across campus in your car seat or stroller and then hope and pray to the dear Lord you didn't cry while I was in class."

My Aunt Jess had married Uncle Travis, my mother's younger brother, and her relationship with my mother had never been a great one. It started off alright when Aunt Jess was fresh out of high school and I wasn't born yet, still encased in my mother's womb. My mother invited Aunt Jess to one of the ultrasound appointments, the one where you get to hear the heartbeat.

"I remember the first moment I loved you. I was at

the doctor with Kim for her ultrasound and we heard your heartbeat. I knew right then my whole world had changed."

My Aunt Jess had a body that was not made to create children of her own. It was my mother's favorite thing to bring up and her favorite weapon to wield, as if her scars and stretch marks were the true markers of motherhood. My mother told Aunt Jess, after she and Uncle Travis adopted my brother and me when we were in high school, that we were just a "paper family" and there was nothing real about that.

It was a knife that buried deep and a wound that festered every time.

There was no one who hated my mother more than Aunt Jess.

No one.

* * *

My mother met Paul at a department store when I was three years old. He was on a ladder, paint scuffing his pants and face as he slicked a coat of white on the walls. They caught each other's eye, fell in love, and nine months later a photo was taken of my mother and Paul in my Nana's living room. She wore overalls and had a round stomach. She had cut her hair to her chin, a look I never preferred, and Paul wore a dark shirt and gelled his black hair back. On the back of the photograph in smeared ink was my Nana's handwriting: "Paul and Kim Wedding, March 1969."

A month later, my brother was born.

"Oh Pumpkin, you just loved your little brother. You thought he was your baby doll. Lordy honey, it was the funniest thing. You would want to dress him up in your baby doll outfits and your dad about had a moose when he walked in one day and Craig was in a sparkly dress. He had the hair for a girl, let me tell you, but no, you just thought he was the grooviest thing."

With Paul came the moving. The bouncing back and forth between Nevada, Arizona, Colorado, Idaho, New Mexico. Always moving, always packing, always leaving Aunt Jess crying on the front porch, always holding the stuffed animals Uncle Travis gave me real close and trying to remember the way *home* smelled.

Before Paul showed up. Before he became a semi-permanent fixture. Before he wrapped his grubby fingers around my mother's hand, my neck and *squeezed*, I hadn't a clue my life was hell. He was a catalyst, a steady flow of gasoline and my mother a flame, ready to burn bright.

Paul worked hard, worked late, worked like it was his religion. Fucked anything with two legs and a pair of tits like it was his religion too. Always made the excuse that he was buried in work when my mother knew he was actually buried inside some "snaggle-toothed whore."

I hated Paul, began hating him when I knew that I could hate someone. I hated him for his cruelty, his absence, his love for my brother and contempt for me. How he would walk around the house fully naked and how he grilled the best burger I had ever eaten.

Late, late one night when I was about eight or so, I woke up to the sound of my mother's screeching and Paul's bellowing. I knew they were fighting and it was scary when they did, but I always had to see. I tiptoed down the hall, the sound of their footsteps thundering through the house.

"I'll do it Paul, I'll *fucking* do it. Don't fucking push me. I swear to God I'll kill your sorry ass."

I had made it to the dining room and crouched in a corner. It was dark with only a lamp in the next room on. It cast an ominous glow and I saw their shadows slinking across the floor before they came into view. Paul shuffled backwards, still in his work attire, a look of pure disgust plastered on his face. My mother, wrapped in a robe, continued to charge after him. I tried to melt into the wall, make myself smaller—invisible. But they didn't see me, too caught up in their rage.

"You psycho bitch," he spat.

My mother stumbled at his words, momentarily thrown off guard before she screamed and charged after him again. Paul sidestepped her, grabbed a handful of her hair, and slammed her into the wall opposite of me. The sharp *crunch* of her nose filled the room. My fingertips zinged. He cursed at her and slammed the door on his way out. I sat frozen in the corner, looking at the crumpled form of my mother and only when she began to stir did I make my way back to my room.

They divorced five years later.

* * *

"I just want to look at her. See what she looks like," I whispered.

My husband grabbed my wrist. His voice shook. "You know that's not a good idea. C'mon, let's just buy this and go."

I looked into his eyes, green as spring leaves. "Please. I'll make it short." I cupped his cheek. "Five minutes."

He glanced over in her direction and his jaw clenched. He sighed. "Five minutes. Then we leave."

I nodded.

* * *

11

There would be times after school when my mother would stumble into the living room, take a long drag of her cigarette before putting it out on the coffee table, and swipe her foot along my ankles, making me fall to the ground. I had just gotten home from a rather lousy day at school when I saw the glassy look in her eyes, saw the bottles and cigarettes strewn across the countertops and knew what was about to happen. I tried to make a run for my room but her foot caught my ankles and I crashed to the floor. My mother moved quick.

She pinned me to the floor. Sitting on my stomach, both her hands were wrapped around my wrists and her knees kept my legs in place. The older I got, the stronger I got which meant the more she had to restrain me but my small ten-year-old body was no match in this position. I squirmed, tried to claw at her hands with my nails, bending and contorting them at odd angles just to barely skim her flesh.

"What's the matter, Pumpkin? Can't move?"

I curled my lip and she *tsked*. She manuerved her body to where her knees held my arms down just long enough to reach behind her and pull off one of her socks. She then wadded it in a ball. I moved my head side to side as quickly as I could but she still managed to shove it in my mouth. I could feel the warmth of it still on my tongue. Taste the days of wear.

My mother moved back to her previous position and began hocking up her spit. She leaned over me and let a thick glob seep between her lips and hang in front of my face. I started to shake my head again. She slurped it back up, laughed, and let it dangle once more, swinging it like a pendulum until it fell right by my nose in a thick, gooey lump and slid across my cheek, on my ear, and into my hair.

My mother was cruel in unusual ways. In the usual ways too. But, my gosh, was she a savant at the unexpected methods of making life miserable. This was her favorite.

It didn't leave bruises.

* * *

My mother dated a slew of men in the 70s and through the early 80s. Most I didn't know since during this time Craig and I were living with Aunt Jess and Uncle Travis. But she would write me letters about how Roger had a slick red Mustang and how Jerry had a son my age and that Mikey could finger the strings of a guitar about as well as he could finger her. She spent a good majority of her time in Mexico when I was fourteen with a man named Jason. I met him a few times before. They always had an on-again, off-again thing and I didn't hate him like I hated Paul.

Jason was quiet, liked to read, wore glasses. He was a nice enough man. We liked to talk about books, Native American history, and The Beatles. Jason didn't make too loud a fuss and really seemed to think my mother was something. He was always sticking up for her and had her back no matter what.

At times, it warmed my heart to know there was one person out there who loved my mother when she had made herself so unloveable.

"Something about that man just doesn't sit right with me," my Aunt Jess said one night while she was painting my nails for a school dance. "He's sort of cowardly. A spineless, no good man that will sit back and watch the world burn before he gets a pail of water to help out. I just don't know how someone could put up with that woman and what she does."

I had sex for the first time when I was sixteen and

13

somehow my mother found out about it. My Aunt Jess drove Craig and me to our mother's for our weekly dinner. The car bounced and shook along the long gravel drive and when my mother's small house came into view, she was standing on the porch smoking a cigarette. Jason sat on a fold-out chair, whittling a chunk of wood.

"Oh boy, looks like she's in a great mood. We're not late, are we?" Craig asked from the backseat.

"Nope," Aunt Jess put the car in park. "Early actually. You two mind your manners and remember who you are, okay? I'll be back to pick you up at seven." As I unbuckled, she leaned over and gave me a quick hug goodbye. She paused for a moment. "Well, good lord, what's she doing?"

My mother threw open my car door. She was mad, *mad* mad. Her brows were furrowed and those two little lines in between them were etched deep. Before I had time to register what was happening, she stubbed her cigarette out on my bare thigh, grabbed a handful of hair at the back of my head, yanked me by it, and threw me to the ground. I could feel the gravel sink into my cheeks, my forehead. Could feel her boot ram into my stomach, my thighs.

I heard my Aunt Jess scream as she tried to get out of the car and make her way to me.

My mother lifted me up off the ground by my hair and I stumbled to my feet, the pain white hot.

"You nasty little whore," she spat at my face, picked up a handful of rocks and threw them at me. They felt like little bullets against my neck, my chest. "You spread your goddamn legs for every little prick that wants in? Huh? Do you, ya filthy cunt?"

I cried. Looked in the car and saw that Craig was crying. Looked at Aunt Jess and saw murder in her eyes. Saw her as she shoved my mother into the side of the car and got real close.

"You don't get to touch my baby! Do you hear me? You don't get to *touch* her." Aunt Jess yelled in her face.

"Why the fuck is *my daughter* sleeping around at sixteen? Do I need to take her back? Raise her under my roof to make sure she's not fucking everything from here to Timbuktu?"

"Kim, you were having sex well before sixteen so don't act holier-than-thou. And don't you dare threaten to take these kids away from me when you haven't done shit for them in years. You cook them one meal a week, Kim. One meal." She held up her index finger. "I'm the one that puts clothes on their backs and takes them to the doctor and makes sure they do well in school and you've only ever played "mommy" when it suits you. So I swear to the dear Lord above if you ever touch one of *my kids* like that again, I'll beat your ass till your head falls off."

My mother looked at me then at Aunt Jess. Her lips snarled and eyes narrowed. "Fuck the both of you. Get the hell off my property." She walked back into her house.

I got in the front seat of the car and picked the tiny bits of gravel from my face. Aunt Jess rested her head on the front of the steering wheel and cried. Craig patted my shoulder.

Jason crossed his legs and waved goodbye.

* * *

I stood next to my mother for a few moments, waiting to see if she would look up at me. My stomach felt heavy, like there was a bowling ball sloshing around and I felt an urge to run. But I was eager to see her. It had been a while.

She shifted uncomfortably before she turned in my direction. Her face was blank, neutral. Her eyes flicked back and forth, looking into mine, trying to register how she knew me, who I was to her. Then —

"Lordy, Pumpkin! I had no idea that was you. My gosh, your hair. So short! I like it."

Her skin had withered. Her hair, though dyed a glossy brown, hung around her face in limp strands. She had put on a little bit of weight which I approved of. Last time I saw her, she was thin and gray. So she was either now eating full meals or not using as bad. Both were victories. But she still reeked of smoke.

"Yeah, I decided to chop it off. Wanted a little bit of a change."

"I feel ya, hon. Say, I haven't had a chance to tell you about . . ." She talked to me in those five minutes about a little bit of everything. All of it concerning her, none of it about what was going on in my life the past few years or how I was. She was like that. Always had been.

I noticed that when she talked she tried to position her head and mouth in a way that covered the fact that she had lost one of her molars. But I had seen it. I didn't bring it up. I wanted to give her that shred of dignity.

My husband waited patiently by the front door. When five minutes hit, he motioned me to come over with a snap of his head. It was time to leave. The conversation had lulled anyway.

"Well, listen. I've got to get going. Still have to cook some dinner."

"Right," she winked at me. "Got to feed our hungry men."

"Right." I scratched the back of my head. "I guess I'll see you at Nana's Christmas this year?"

"Oh yeah, I'll be there."

"Okay then."

She gave me a hug, the stench of smoke billowing out of her clothes when she pressed against me. "I love you so much. I'll see you later."

I pulled back and looked at her face. She was not beautiful anymore. She was tired, sick—wilted almost. She was a photo that had sat out in the sun too long whose colors were bleached. A flower that was dried up and laid in the pages of a book. She was full of hatred, poisoned by narcissism and a skewed sense of reality. A woman who liked to see others hurt by her hands and words. Loved to see the power she held there. A woman who never wanted to be a mother, not wholly and not in the ways that mattered, and found ways to make me pay for the crime I committed when I stripped her freedom from her.

She was a lonely wretch and, God, did it show in her eyes.

"We have to lie in the beds we make," Aunt Jess told me. "You can't be a selfish, nasty person to everyone and expect them to want to be around you. Just isn't how the world works. Kim can't have her cake and eat it too. She did this to herself."

My heart broke for her. It always did.

Probably always would no matter how horrible she'd been.

* * *

I remember one night when I was little, maybe five, I found my mother face down in a pool of her own vomit again. A glass of amber liquid lay nearby and a few bottles of beer littered the linoleum. I pinched my nose and shook her shoulders.

"Mama," I whispered. "Get up, Mama. Craig is fussy and Daddy's not home."

She groaned and slowly sat up, leaning against the fridge. She took her shirt off and wiped her mouth with it.

She wasn't wearing a bra underneath. Her hands smoothed her hair back, picked the chunks out of the front strands.

"I love you, Pumpkin." Her voice sounded jumbled, like her tongue was swollen and her mouth was full of marbles. "Curly head and all, I love you."

"I love you too, Mama."

"C'mere," she slurred. "Let me hold you for a second." I shimmied into her lap, careful not to touch her vomit next to us. "You're my best friend, Pumpkin. You really are. You know when you were a little bitty baby I'd strap you in the car seat, roll the windows down, and we'd cruise till we couldn't cruise no more. Those were the best days. Just the two of us."

I nodded.

"The best days," she mumbled.

I sat in her lap until she fell asleep again, head resting against the white of the fridge and mouth hung wide open.

I curled up in bed with Craig that night leaving my mother alone in the middle of the mess she'd made herself.

———————————————

Paige E. Reecer is an aspiring author with a Master of Arts in Creative Writing who just finished her first novel earlier this year. Knowing from the age of eight that she wanted to be a writer, Paige has spent years staring at computer screens and scratching away on paper trying to bring life to the stories and characters that live in her head that she holds near to her heart. When she is not devoting hours to editing her book and drafting its sequel, she's reading copious amounts of romance novels, giving her kitty cat Xavier all the pets, or singing "Phantom of the Opera" to herself in her mirror.

Two Poems
by Elizabeth Hill

A Summer's Day, For Comparison

A speckled sun shimmers off seas and sails,
a miasma of light and saline warmth.
Children in the snowy sand fill their pails
while the cerulean sea glints and froths.
Some racing sailboats leisurely pass buoys.
The sailors leaning back to revel in
the ocean's spray are happy and boozy.
Below, the sparkling bright fish glide and grin.
Glad gulls exchanging jokes cackle and strut
on bobbing rocks which dance amidst the din.
Fair cumulus clouds puff over the gut,
suspended by the sultry, lazy wind.
A single prop plane sputters 'neath the clouds,
towing a banner with "EAT AT McDOWD'S."

The Northeast Wind

One morning, at thirteen,
she woke with the promise
of the northeast wind.
She heard the faint clanking of the rigging
hitting the aluminum mast of the family boat.
Out the window, the sun flickered
on the young leaves of birches,
which rustled like crinkling paper.
The cerulean sea peeped through the trees,
framed as if by a child's intricate cut-out.
Blue nuthatches speckled the air with their
chipper calls. She softly padded
onto the front porch in her nightgown
and looked out over the sparse grass
to the bluff and scraggly pitch pines which held it up.
Beyond the bluff, their small sailboat
lightly bobbed on miniature waves
caused by the bright northeast wind.
She made a plan to sample yesterday's
blueberry bread before anyone woke up.
Then, stretching her arms out like a cross,
she breathed deeply, filling her lungs
with readiness. Life was wide open.
Yesterday's complications had vanished.
Her whole family was asleep.
These rare, new moments were hers alone.
She took off her nightgown and
walked down the path, strewn with stones,
to the rocky beach. Picking her way across
stones and shells, she entered the water.
She walked out, neck deep, and ducked under.

Then, rising up from under the salt water,
thrusting to the surface, she arrived,
gleeful, blessed and new.

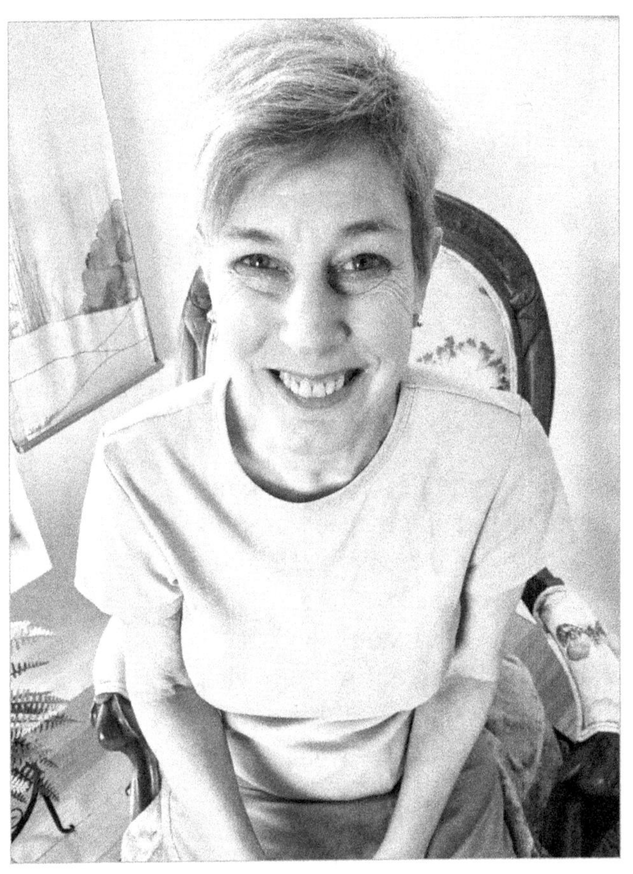

Elizabeth Hill is a retired lawyer. She was an Administrative Law Judge, deciding suits between learning disabled children and the school system. She lives in Harlem, NYC with her husband and two irascible cats. Hill grew up in New Hampshire and on Cape Cod. She is an avid walker and enjoys Pilates. Her work is soon to be published in 34th Parallel Magazine *and* Blue Lake Review. *She writes poetry in the hope that others who read it will share the feelings she expresses. She also writes because she loves words and the process of choosing just the right ones to convey a feeling or thought.*

Three Poems
by Cameron Morse

Parent Teacher

Night of the meeting I scrunch into my
child-sized chair and get ready
for a talking to. In the empty classroom,
two women have been waiting
for a while. The full moon idles out
in the silent parking lot. I want to wipe
the spider webs out of their eyes,
these ladies of the night. I want to tell them
a good story that will whisk us off
to sleep. Another parent is always backed up
behind, laying on an angry horn.
I would prefer to hover an inch above
the pavement. Slam on the brakes,
daybreak. Caterwauling makes my skin crawl.

Jixian

Where the body finds itself at home
in the bright seam of afternoon, I have
afternooned in brightness, crossing
a dusty intersection of tuk-tuks
toward a prayer tree in the temple yard
in Jixian. Ribbons lifting lightly, yes,
and eaves which wasps cruise, but also
inside that warm palm the chill blade

of a breeze has again suggested a double
edge to my happiness: a cold coin
in the alms bowl of the sun. Whether the idea
is spring, or sprung, or autumn, God knows.
I know only I am at ease in my body:
My body thinks it's OK to stay here a while.

Me and my Children

Boy with the cereal box on your head,
girl with the cheesy grin, window
in the shape of a fan ablaze, a blazing window,
I am a mote of dust in the kitchen
that is lit at sunrise and otherwise invisible
in my own life. Bacon smoke, the smell
of ground coffee and the screech of the grinding.
My children are the wind that kicks up
the window curtain. Toppling garbage cans
up and down the block. The squirrels that disfigure
a perfect pumpkin. They are board meetings
of stuffed animals, top bunk aerial photographs
of squiggly train tracks while I, always,
am just the eye behind the lens.

Cameron Morse is Senior Review editor at Harbor Review *and the other of eight collections of poetry. His first collection,* Fall Risk, *won Glass Lyre Press's 2018 Best Book Award. His latest is* The Thing Is *(Briar Creek Press, 2021). He holds an MFA from the University of Kansas City-Missouri and lives in Independence, Missouri, with his wife Lili and their three children. For more information, check out his Facebook page or website:* cameronmorsepoems.wordpress.com

————————

Fragments of Longing
by Bharti Bansal

I am just a touch away from dissolving.
A little nudge, a little tug at the hem of my shirt,
perhaps a handshake that turns into a hug,
or just a small confession at the altar of my heart.
There are not enough gods who aren't hungry,
so carry me in your frail arms and feed me to them,
like an offering/apology
I, for once, want to be desired even if it means death.

Look at my eyes, see for yourself that there aren't enough traces
left by memorable laughter that can convince me into staying.

But here I am,
still surviving like a Beatles' song, or perhaps a school prayer
where the voices of others save you from your own.

I want to be saved like a flower on the sidewalk
but these fragments of longing, worn fibers of an old blanket
which smells like the past, are too visible to hide.
So I pull them apart, one by one
until the cold eats me. Winter never ends
for people who know burning as love,
and there aren't enough rivers to carry the ashes,
not enough people who know that the only thing
separating water and us is the ability
to come back home.

Bharti Bansal is a twenty-four-year old poet from India. Her work has appeared in magazines like Aaduna, Live Wire India, Feminism in India, two drops of ink, The Sunflower Collective, *and is forthcoming in the anthology,* The Yearbook of Indian Poetry.

Ian Walkley

A Father's Son
by Sandeep Kumar Mishra

The mourners were not plentiful the day of the funeral. Vasudev had not been a popular man in this life, having dedicated very little time to cultivating and maintaining relationships. Pradeep, his eldest, watched the people move about in respectful silence, occasionally stopping at one of his siblings or mother to offer quiet condolences while the chanters continued through their mantras. Some made their way over to him, but he had nothing to say to them in return. Everything was too fresh—Pradeep wasn't sure how he felt about his father's death yet. He hadn't even seen his father for at least ten years before now, having gone off to live with his aunt while still a boy.

He looked over at his mother, his brother Ishaan, and his sister Shaleena. His mother looked sad at least, but Ishaan and Shaleena looked about as numb as he doubtless did. He wondered what the past ten years had been like for them. If their father had changed at all since failing Pradeep.

He would never forget the first time his father struck him. It was a miserable, humid day, the air so wet that you could almost taste it. Vasudev was home, classes having been let out, and was especially short of temper.

Pradeep, still a small child at the time, refused to go outside to play. "It's too hot," he remembered protesting. "I'll melt!"

His mother had gently but firmly encouraged him to

go outside anyway. "You won't melt, I promise. But you really should go outside. The sun is good for you."

"I don't want to!" His little voice rose in aggravation.

"Pradeep, my darling, please go outside." His mother looked around, fear coloring her face. It was the first time Pradeep could recall seeing his mother afraid, though it would not be the last.

Vasudev appeared around the corner, his face an oncoming storm, and Pradeep instinctively understood his mother's fear.

"What is the meaning of this noise?" It was less a question than a demand.

Pradeep ventured a reply. "I don't want to go outside."

The baleful gaze Vasudev leveled at his son burned into the young boy's soul. "I heard your mother tell you to go outside. Why do you stand there mewing?"

"I—"

SLAP.

"Do as you're told! If I see you in the house again before supper you will get twice as bad!"

"I know your father was not a kind man." Pradeep shook his head, returning to the moment, and looked over to his Aunt Shashi. "Perhaps he will be kinder in next life."

Pradeep couldn't reply to that. He wasn't certain his father deserved another life.

"I am sorry you did not get to say goodbye," his aunt ventured again. She was a kind woman, almost a second mother to Pradeep, but she was too forgiving.

"I am not." The first words Pradeep had spoken since the funeral began. "We spent all our words to each other a long time ago."

A young Pradeep stood nervously in his father's cramped office. Their small house afforded little enough space for their steadily growing family, yet Vasudev refused to give up this room. Pradeep had no idea what it was for, he just knew that his father's claims to it meant that he and his new brother Ishaan would be sharing a room.

"Your brother will be your responsibility," he remembered his father saying sternly, eyes intense and hard. "I expect you to pull your weight as the eldest."

Pradeep didn't speak. He knew by then that discussions with his father were not truly discussions, they were just brief moments when his father bothered to remember he had a child long enough to impart specific instructions. Any words on Pradeep's part would earn him a backhand, and that was if his father was in a decent mood.

"That means helping your mother feed and change him, teach him, and—"

"Keep him out of your way?"

The words were a mistake—Pradeep knew that before he said them, but sometimes he couldn't help himself. He stood defiantly as the fury entered his father's eyes. He would feel the repercussions of that remark for a long time, and remember them even longer.

Pradeep wasted no time after the traditional ten day mourning period to get back to his life. The fact that he even had to take ten whole days off irritated him, and he was unreasonably short with his family because of it. He wanted to leave this house and its memories, wanted to get back to his wife and children and wanted to burn the past away just as the body had been burned.

By sunrise on the eleventh day he was packed and ready to go, not even staying for breakfast. He bore no resentment towards his mother or siblings, but they had lived the past ten years without him; there was no reason to stay here any longer. So he quickly and quietly slipped out of the home of his childhood to catch the first train of the day and refused to look back.

As he walked, his thoughts wandered. He looked forward to home, hoped the train was running on time, hoped his wife Viha had set aside some dinner for him, and a thousand other thoughts like these—anything to get his mind off where he was and what had just happened and get him moving forward. He was so focused on putting the past behind him that he didn't notice the football until it was almost too late.

With a small yelp he bobbed his head to the side, narrowly avoiding a head-on collision with the flying ball. He shook his head, startled and confused, and looked around for the ball's owner. He spotted them easily enough, a young boy—who was smiling apologetically—and his father—who was laughing—just down the road. The father jogged towards Pradeep.

"My apologies," he began, still laughing a little. "My son and I like to come out for a little game before I have to go to work, and we are unaccustomed to sharing the road so early."

Pradeep took a moment to gather his wits before answering. "Ah... it is alright. I was not hit, so no harm." His eyes drifted back to the boy. "You two do this... often?"

The father nodded. "Most mornings. I work long hours, so I cherish the moments I can. Surely you can understand this?"

Pradeep looked back at the father. Such genuine happiness, speaking about his son, was something Pradeep did not understand at all.

"Pradeep, why does father never come out to play with us?"

Pradeep didn't turn to look at his little sister. Shaleena was barely five, but already she was noticing that their house was not like the houses of some of her friends. Her father was practically a stranger to her, only seen at meals and on holidays. No great loss there, Pradeep thought with no small measure of distaste.

"Because he is too busy," Ishaan said when it was obvious that Pradeep had nothing to say.

"Busy with what?"

Ishaan paused. "Work, I guess."

Shaleena clearly didn't understand, but filed the information away nonetheless and pressed on to her next question. "And why is he so sad?"

This got Pradeep to speak. "You think he's sad?" Shaleena nodded and Pradeep scoffed. "Why do you think this?"

"Because he never smiles. Sad people don't smile."

It made sense, in a little kid logic sort of way, but Pradeep had trouble picturing his father's constantly dour expression as anything but angry.

"He isn't sad," Pradeep said finally, frowning at the football by his feet. "I don't know what he is, but he isn't sad."

This confused the little girl more but Pradeep chose that moment to kick the ball and she took off after it, screaming with joy. Ishaan looked at Pradeep and frowned. "You should not speak of our father like that."

Pradeep just rolled his eyes and watched Shaleena run.

Given the early hour the train station was thankfully quiet, and Pradeep managed to purchase his ticket and board with minimal wait. He also had his choice of seats for the long ride ahead of him. Settling his luggage above him, he sat heavily and sighed, thankful to be on the way home at last. The rest of his day promised to be an easy one, as it was nothing more tedious than waiting until he reached his stop that evening, then getting a cab to take him home. Comforted by these thoughts, he drifted into a light nap as the train began to move.

When he stirred a few hours later, he noticed the car was significantly more crowded than it had been, with nearly all the seats outside of the one directly beside him taken. He also noticed a lone man who, noticing that Pradeep was awake, headed his way.

"A thousand apologies, sir, but is that seat taken?" He indicated the seat beside Pradeep.

"No. Please, sit." The man nodded his thanks and situated his own luggage, pulling out a well-worn book before stashing the bags, and settled into the seat. Pradeep's eyes were instantly drawn to the cover.

The man noticed Pradeep's attention and held the book up for better inspection. "I take it you are familiar with "*Songs of Kabir*"?"

Pradeep startled at the man's question as though shocked. "Oh, ah, not as such. Or rather I have not taken the time to read that particular collection myself. Someone... I knew, they did. Spoke of it very highly."

The man nodded understandingly and began flipping through the pages. "It is a good book. If you have any love of poetry, I highly recommend it."

"I... shall keep that in mind."

"What are you reading?"

Pradeep looked up from his own perch across the room from the conversation, watching where Shaleena had approached their father's armchair and interrupted his reading with her question. He instinctively tensed, waiting for the cold dismissal or fiery rage at being disturbed; the first would cause Shaleena to run away hurt and Pradeep to follow so he could calm her down, and the second would be directed at Pradeep for not keeping her distracted in the first place. Either way it was about to become Pradeep's problem.

Yet Vasudev did neither. Instead, he looked up slowly and studied his daughter for a moment, as though trying to remember who she was and how he should react. Then he closed—actually closed—his book in order to show her the cover. "This is a book of poems. Can you read the title?"

Shaleena squinted at the letters. "*Songs of Kabir*"?" She spoke slowly, careful to get every word correct. Pradeep couldn't help but be a little impressed. He hadn't realized her reading skills had progressed so far.

Vasudev smiled at her, and Pradeep frowned in confusion. "That's right," their father said, sounding pleased. "Would you like to read some poems with me?"

Pradeep looked back down to his own book, but he couldn't focus on the words anymore. That was the kindest he'd ever seen his father behave towards anyone outside of their mother. Poems, it seemed, were the only subject he could be approached with. Something to remember.

Hailing a taxi to take him from the train station to his home didn't take long, thankfully. It was already much later than Pradeep had hoped to arrive home, and he was anxious for the comfort of his wife and bed. As he was driven across the city, the driver made occasional attempts at small talk, most of which Pradeep answered with polite but short replies, doing his best to avoid a protracted conversation. One comment, however, caused him to pay attention.

"Are you excited for the start of Onam tomorrow?"

Pradeep blinked. "That's tomorrow?"

The driver nodded. "I love Onam, personally. Well, specifically the Onasadya Feast, but the entire festival is fun." Pradeep glanced at the driver's bulky figure and guessed that the man did not save feasting for the festival alone. "Do you participate?"

"Hurry, Pradeep! Father wants us to be among the first visitors to the temple!"

Pradeep groaned, stretched, and tried to rub the sleep from his eyes. "The... temple?"

"Yes, the temple!" Shaleena was entirely too excited and loud for this early hour. "It's the first day of Onam!"

Pradeep shook himself more fully away and swung his legs over the side of his bed. Onam... he smiled a little as Shaleena scampered off, her mission accomplished. Father was always in high spirits during religious festivals and holy days, his usual dour expression lightened and stormy mood calmed. He might even be persuaded to give his children treats, so long as all the proper observances are met. "It is a holy day first and a festival second," he would solemnly intone. "Be respectful of that."

And they were, though it was more out of fear of their father than respect for the day. Still, it bought the household some peace, and at the time it seemed worth it.

Pradeep slipped quietly into his home, unsure if his wife was still awake and knowing their infant son was not. He paused just inside, seeing the flower decorations all prepared for Onam. Setting his luggage down in the entryway and taking off his shoes to make as little noise as possible, he made a quick walk of the house.

Everything was spotless. His wife had done an excellent job keeping up with the cleaning, even with the added responsibility of their newborn. He smiled slightly as he paused by the dining room table, laying a hand on their son's highchair. *She is a good woman. I hope I am a good husband to her.* He wondered briefly if his father ever had the same concern.

He moved into his office and saw everything was just as he had left it. It was, by agreement, the only room she didn't routinely clean, as Pradeep had his own method to the seeming madness. He knew where everything was and that was the important part. He looked over his papers, his bookshelf, the grading pens and the half-finished poems, and he frowned. It looked remarkably like how he remembered his father's office being laid out.

How had he never noticed that before? "Am I becoming my father...?" The question was asked quietly, barely even whispered, as though Pradeep was afraid of the answer. In a way he was; were not all men their fathers' sons? What hope did he have to build a better life for himself when he mirrored his father in even this tiny detail? In what other ways had he shaped himself after a man he... he what?

He missed. Here, in the darkness and the silence, he could admit it. He missed his father. Or, perhaps put better, he missed the idea of his father. He missed the connection he saw so often, even just coming home from the funeral. Someone he could talk to, someone he could play ball with, someone who led by example and listened to the worries of his children. Vasudev had never been any of those things for Pradeep, but he'd seen glimpses of that man in the way Shaleena interacted with him, and wondered if he had changed at all after Pradeep had left. If he had missed his son as much as his son now missed him.

"It's too late for regrets," Pradeep told his ghosts, trying to push them away. "He's dead. Whatever that may mean for him, it means to me that he is beyond reach." Forgiveness and healing were beyond Pradeep's reach; there was no saving Vasudev's memory or salvaging the relationship. The abuse, the neglect, and the fear were all Pradeep had to remember his father by.

Pradeep left his office and its ghosts and headed up the stairs. He paused midway up to look at the pictures hanging from the wall—him and his wife on vacation, on their wedding day, on the day they brought their son home for the first time. They were happy in those pictures. Pradeep knew true joy in every moment captured and it showed. He thought back to pictures of his father; Vasudev had rarely smiled in person and never for the camera. Even in the oldest photos he looked serious and stoic, never expressing joy in his life.

He finished climbing the stairs, bypassing his own bedroom to check on his son. The child was sleeping soundly, completely oblivious to the presence of his father, and Pradeep smiled down at the small bundle. Resting a hand on the side of the crib and nearly crying for reasons he couldn't explain, he made his son a promise. "I'll do better. I swear, I will do better."

The floor creaked softly, and Pradeep looked over his shoulder to see his wife, wrapped in her dressing robe, squinting sleepily at him. "Pradeep?" Her voice was barely audible, and he quietly crept over to her after a final look at his son. "I didn't hear you come in." She squinted at him again, then reached out and touched his face, concern taking over her expression. "You're crying! What's wrong?"

Pradeep cupped her hand and smiled. "Nothing. Come, let us go back to bed. I am ready for today to end and tomorrow to begin."

Sandeep Kumar Mishra is a Bestseller author of One Heart- Many Breaks-2020. *An outsider artist, a poet and a lecturer. He is a guest poetry editor at* Indian Poetry Review. *He has received "Readers Favorite Silver Award-21", "Indian Achievers Award-21", IPR Annual Poetry Award-2020 and Literary Titan Book Award-2020. He was shortlisted for "2021 International Book Awards", "Indies Today Book of the Year Award 2020", "Joy Bale Boone Poetry Prize 2021" and "Oprelle Rise up Poetry Prize 2021". He was also "The Story Mirror Author of the Year" nominee-2019.*

Why Moment
by Eugene Donaldson

Beneath our feet flow subterranean rivers,
water highways hidden in our earth's body.
They rush, rumble, and twist through dark rock,
independent of the bounding waters above.

Did you know a tea salesman unintentionally
invented the tea bag, making himself wealthy?
So rich, his family could not spend all
their money in a lifetime of joy.

Inventions & discoveries can make millions—
no, billions of dollars. Think, water slides,
tearless onion slicers, weight-loss formulas,
naming stars. Think progress. Think canniness.

"Birdseye" was a man, not a logo on a brand
of frozen vegetables. He studied Arctic frogs,
experimented with food and the way frogs
make it through long winter months.

Velcro duplicates how Nature propagates
in the fields. Cockeburs and beggars' lice,
seeds that stick to animals' fur and hikers'
denim pants. In my *why moment,* my lit

candle of curiosity, I ask whether the Pacific
can be siphoned onto land, making it available
to the firefighters of combustible California.
Imagine–if not the ocean's salty waters,

why not those underground rivers going
nowhere? After all, beneath the forests' roots
the mycelium acts like the internet moving
sustainable data about, keeping our earth alive.

———————————————

Eugene Donaldson began his creative journey with a BA in Fine Arts from the University of Maryland. He has contributed to Blue Moon Literary & Art Review *since 2018. He was a finalist in the Jimenez-Porter Literary Prize 2020 (University of Maryland).*

Thinking Just A Little of Aristotle in the Evening
by Terence John

Dressed in the skin of an old man
I remain essential to *myself*
All's still functioning
north and south
I still applaud all my decisive moods
the ghostly cheroot still holds me in its mouth
I've conquered
love by surrendering to it
becoming my own victim in a pleasurable way
I stay close to nature
the wisest part of me my lover says
and haughty swaying threshing sycamores
in the wind agree
Nico agrees while vacuuming his Island Lake bar
and I agree
when watching the sun go down
over Wasagamack
smelling pine smoke over water
hearing a mockingbird sing

Terence John's poetry has been published extensively throughout Europe and the United States, in the following journals: Southlight, Acumen, The London Magazine, Orbis, The North, The Poetry Review, Poetry Salzburg Review, Stand, Sarasvati, The Pomegranate London, Blue Moon Literary & Art Review, Glasgow Review of Books, *and online worldwide at medium.com San Francisco/*The Nonconformist Magazine.

Bathroom Wall
by Roger Singer

on the
bathroom wall
of a dingy
unnamed gas station
at the corner
of routes 66 and 716
in the company
of stains and decay
graffiti spreads
and blossoms;

half drawn faces
copied hand prints
acid revelations
a lipstick kiss
phone numbers
skeleton heads
Paul is dead

last testaments
from lost spirits
on the run

Dr. Singer is a Poet Laureate Emeritus of Connecticut, and past president of the Connecticut Shoreline Poetry Chapter, in association with the Connecticut Poetry Society. He has had over 1,350 poems published on the internet, magazines and in books and is a 2017 Pushcart Prize Award Nominee.

Go with the World
by David Lloyd Sutton

Once upon a time there was a boy named Paco who herded goats in the Santa Rosas.

And one day a neopuma came and took a particularly fine, soft-eared nanny of whom Paco was very fond.

It happened that on that same day a hunter from the new government in Los Angeles came to Paco's village.

He said that he had very fine guns and machines for just such problems. Paco would show him the area and he, the official hunter, would rid them of the neopuma.

This was a nice thing. The new government had so far only sent tax collectors to Paco's village. They were lucky, having a small gold-bearing stream, and so they hadn't had to give up livestock or corn, like the other villages. The gold would have bought good wrought iron, or steel, or stout hickory for tool handles, though, and it *was* nice to get something for it after all. They were all very interested in seeing how the official hunter would go about his job.

The first day was very interesting. The hunter had a machine he said could *smell*. With this contrivance on his back, its pickup boom in one hand and a beautiful rifle in the other, he accompanied Paco and the goats into the high foothills. The hunter was a strong looking young man, but he was sweating fiercely by the end of the first long slope.

Paco wondered *why* a machine that had to be carried rather than a dog which could carry itself. None of the village dogs would follow a neopuma, of course, but surely the government could train one to do so.

It was warm, the season early fall, and it would be fiercely hot by midmorning. Paco took his flock into oaks, where they would be cool, and where he could amble along cross-slope, not having to fight the bush.

The hunter left them where the kill had occurred the day before. He wanted Paco to come with him, but Paco explained that a goatherd was really part of the flock. He must stay where the goats were cool.

They did not see the hunter again for three days. Then, in late evening, he limped in, his clothing in tatters, his fine smelling machine smashed, his beautiful rifle pitifully scraped and scratched. They were too polite, in the way of the Santa Rosas, to question him, but that night he told them of two days of cross canyon scrambling, during which he had found only the remnants of the stolen goat. The neopuma had ambushed him then, knocking him over a rockfall, ruining the machine, then vanishing.

They all nodded. Neopumas were very smart. Of course, none of them would follow such a beast to a blind spot, but this fellow was apparently very brave. They fed him and the women brought many basins of hot water for his swollen feet.

Two more days, and Paco lost another goat. The hunter decided to find the kill and sit up on it. He ate a hearty dinner and set off. All of the men shook their heads, but all agreed that they must not be too sure, yet.

In the morning, however, Paco found the hunter, as expected, bandaged him, and took the flock home to get stretcher bearers.

The headman was sad, as they all were. He told Paco, "You must do it yourself, boy. It is interesting, true, to watch this official hunter, but we cannot afford another goat."

"*Si, bueno, Jefe*, but could I use his good rifle? I do not like to use a one-shot or a bow for neopuma."

"*Por que no*? He is unconscious, and he brought it to use on our problems."

Thus it was, that when the official hunter became conscious several days later, he woke to see Paco carefully scraping a neopuma hide, its lustrous purple fur spilling over half the hut.

"But... *how*?"

I *did* borrow your very fine rifle."

"Even so. *How*?"

"You must go *with* the world."

"How so?"

"A man does not have to walk cross-canyon. He can climb high and go down-canyon much faster."

"Did you?"

"No, neopumas always make it very hard to follow them."

"Did you sit up on a kill?"

"Not quite... and I would not do so without fasting for several days, eating the leaves of sage, swimming in running water, . . . "

"**ENOUGH**! How did you kill it?!"

The small boy grinned and held up the hunter's own rifle and one used cartridge.

"But..."

Paco grinned still more.

"I went *with* the big *gato*. I used catnip!"

David Lloyd Sutton has written magazine articles on topics ranging from martial arts to horses to firearms. His short work has appeared repeatedly in Community of Voices, *an anthology associated with the Santa Barbara Writers' Conference. Since moving into novel-length work he has published a western,* Big Hills, *and two sci-fis,* Longest Run *and* Dominus.

Ian Walkley

Three Poems
by Gayle Jansen Beede

59 Karmann Ghia

Inspired by George Bilgere's poem, "'56 Corvette"
and by word prompts:
bones, yellow, ten, clock, stretch, electrical, mask

If pale blue sky were green
it would be the tone
of Dad's Karmann Ghia.
The bones of it seem almost hollow,
like a bird's, so easy it is to drive,
which I do as often as he lets me.
I practice shifting gears in parking lots
before braving the hills of Hacienda Heights
en route to L.A. with a girlfriend to buy
incense and candles at Olvera Street,
those kind that drip down
all over the fancy Italian wine bottles:
stalactites of rainbow-colored wax.
Nights, doing homework together while
spinning some Phil Ochs or Joni Mitchell
on the turntable, we muse
about how to rush through these
wretched teen years, oblivious

to our bodies' ticking clocks,
not yet realizing *now* is where it's at.
Not yet knowing that life
with a capital L only
gets harder than conquering acne,
pulling all-nighters cramming,
dissecting some poor frog,
having to solve for X and Y, and
proving, in a thousand words or less,
that the themes of loneliness
and alienation run rampant in
Catcher in the Rye. It sucks,
going another long week without
having a steady, ready to give
our eye teeth to be winding mohair
around some boy's class ring
so that it fits on our finger.
Stretched before us like a fix, though,
is the weekend: electrical in its allure
of sleeping in and Cocoa Butter
and glassy, primo waves,
tanned buff boys riding
the surf at Huntington Beach.
We'll crank our transistors all the way up–
hoping to hear "Summer in the City"
or "Mellow Yellow," our new faves–
and spend babysitting money
on Big Hunks and Pepsi Colas
sold in the snack shack
near Lifeguard Station # 10.
We take our flat stomachs,
long wavy hair, and lithe legs for granted.
With luck, two of those buff surfer boys
will see *us* amidst the crowded shore

of golden, prone bikini-clad girls
catching rays on the sand.
If they do, maybe we'll make up
fake names like Bonnie or Bridgette
to go along with the other lies
we'll tell them, masking our silly jitters.
With luck, we won't forget our wallets
at the beach or to sweep the sand out
of Dad's immaculate Ghia,
knowing how much it bugs him.

Body Language

Is vocabulary anchored
to the current that buoys
my mother's body,

eerie, slo-mo writhing
as though she's drowning
on the sheets? Reverend Biology

is delivering a final tirade
of synapses and strictures,
closing down the beautiful

well-oiled vessel that once
housed me in undulant
aquatic perfection.

Someone has brought her
two paper butterflies
with turquoise and golden wings,

appearing like Fine Art
next to the meek, white-bread
sandwich suffocating in cellophane

on a slate gray tray
with broth, pudding, and
a mound of something mashed.

Are you hungry?
What can I do for you?
Are you in pain?

I echo words she often spoke
to me, shedding her needs
like someone molting. Like

butterflies themselves,
nurses come and go in attentive flurry,
talking about how much we need

the rain that's pelting the windows
of the hospital room, the storm
morphing rigid palm trees

into a sopping wet hula dance.
I try to summon a smile
while I hold my mother's hand

looking into her wandering brown eyes,
struggling to decipher
what her moans mean.

I gaze out blurred panes,
remembering so very,
very much— in particular,

her thoroughly flawless dives
into the Stanislaus River
when she was thirty-something

on summer vacation,
where in tingly cold water
she would be submerged,

invisible for the longest time
in alluring emerald waters,
how she would emerge unfazed

as though she were made of gills
and fins and ample oxygen,
undeniably equipped

for going under,
coming up,
going under again.

This Brief Captivity

In a dimly lit exam room
the ultrasound tech tells me
her name is Ai, meaning *love*
in her native tongue, Vietnamese.
She helps me on with the paper gown,
activates the machinery, and
glides warmed goo along my arm,
all the way up to my neck.
I glance over at the screen,
noticing how something looks
like the surface of the moon,
something else like marbleized meat.
I envy her knowledge. She knows
exactly what to look for,
the indicatory and the mystery.

I'm old enough to remember
our countries' shared history,
coming of age years before
her wartime birth. Trembling
intermittently from nerves,
I relinquish any authority over my body,
prone on this gurney in the dark,
the riverlike map-work of my veins
under the medical experts' scrutiny.
Science, I trust, will have the answer;
I'll lose sleep waiting for it.
Easy to want stars as opposed
to the pocked, bone-colored ceiling
I stare at, the faint tick-tock of the clock
far less audible than my drumming heart
as the wand hunts for a clot.

You have decent veins, she tells me,
I bet it's dissolved. Is that buoyancy
in her voice? *Decades of running*, I say.
Maybe it helped. And now I close my eyes
and lie still in this brief captivity,
letting her complete her work,
mesmerized by the whoosh of technology,
yet my mind strays. I can't help but wonder
about Ai's escape from her war-torn land,
and want to ask what gave her the strength?
I think of my husband, not at war
like so many Ukrainian men
but out there in the waiting room,
making small talk or scrolling weather.com.
Like water finding low ground
are my thoughts, survivor's guilt
steering them. *All finished*, she announces,
wiping my arm dry. With the pandemic,
hugging someone isn't wise,
but her job's done, and Ai accepts mine,
returning it with all of her small body,
its flesh warm, its bones strong.
Ban se on thoi, she says. *You'll be fine.*

Gayle Jansen Beede is at work on her first novel, Little Bones. *Some of her poetry has appeared in* Art/Life, Eclipse, Karamu, Piker Press, Poet & Critic, Spectrum, Zone 3, *and others. She is* Blue Moon's *Poetry Editor and the author of* You Can Practically See Cattle Dancing, Audrey to Zoe: An Alphabet of Critters, *and* The Beautiful Culprit. *After an array of gigs in restaurants, graphic arts, editing and public relations, Gayle worked in the field of healthcare in Santa Barbara for over twenty-five years. She now lives in the East Bay in northern California.*

Loyalty
by Lauren Mesa

*In 1942 the US government assembled and shipped
off to concentration camps 112,000 men, women, and
children, the entire Japanese American population of
the three Pacific Coast states.*

Like gentle horses, they arrive every morning
wearing the getas their fathers made:
clop clop, clop clop. The wooden shoes
protect them from infection
that is everywhere around camp.

My classroom is a barracks,
the desks rough plywood. Tea-colored faces
turn up eagerly for roll call,
hands that are curled together
like poised lilies raise.

One student tells me her grandfather
built the California railroad. Another's uncle
broke farm soil all around Sacramento,
and someone's family owned a thriving grocery.
He smiles at the adjectives *plump* and *ripe*.

Outside our classroom their parents
walk by with shovels and picks.
Looking over rows of black heads
bent at arithmetic, I think
of the earth their parents

have just turned.
I walk to my car, passing
windows that appear candlelit
where slender onions grow
flame-like in bowls.

———————————————

Lauren Mesa is the author and illustrator of Homeward, *for young and old, about the Paradise Camp Fire animals, and* Beholding, *a devotional for Advent. Both are available on Amazon. Her poetry has been published in many literary journals, including* Poetry *and* The Laurel Review. *Lauren is a ceramic artist living in Chico, Ca, known as the "city of trees."*

Ian Walkley

The Forgotten Epidemic
by Anne Da Vigo

The patients lay in dim, spare, scoured rooms. Their arms and legs—thin shafts of inert skin and bone—were hidden by white bedspreads. Iron lungs crouched on their chests and hissed. These men and women were the forgotten—victims of polio.

In 1955, I saw them once a week as a volunteer at a suburban Denver nursing home. That was the year I turned fourteen, the year I got an injection of Dr. Jonas Salk's vaccine.

The recent Covid-19 epidemic stirred memories—how our lives in those times were impacted by polio.

I arrived at the nursing home about 4:30 in the afternoon with my schoolbooks heavy in the crook of my arm. A particular smell—fish sticks and Pinesol—assaulted my nose as soon as I stepped inside. The halls were empty, and my laces clicked against the tops of my saddle shoes.

I hung up my car coat and stashed my books in the pantry, then changed into a white blouse and pinafore with patch pockets.

Now dressed in uniform, I pushed through the swinging doors into the kitchen, its enameled cabinets yellow from years of greasy cooking smoke.

"You're here. Good." The cook waved a large spoon and turned back to dishing up dinner. He slid the trays into a tall metal rack on wheels, each slot labeled with a patient's room number. I helped the nurses push the rack down the halls, deliver the meals, and feed the patients.

"Oops. Sorry. Excuse me." I was clumsy, but the more I practiced, the fewer patients had food splashed on their faces and nightgowns. When I missed, I blotted the spills with napkins tucked under their chins like babies' bibs. Milk and coffee were less likely to dribble. The patients sucked the liquids through straws that I threaded between their lips.

They talked to me over the noise of the iron lung, turning their head and wrinkling a cheek against the pillow. Even the patients in the oscillating beds talked as their bodies dipped and rose to the rhythm of the motor: about food, the weather, my school, but never about polio. They seemed old, but thinking back now, I hear young voices, people in their twenties.

The seesawing beds mirrored my mood during those evenings. I felt disoriented, as if I were walking on a sidewalk that tilted at a strange angle. In my white-bread neighborhood, I was sheltered from people who lived on the edge of life.

Unwed pregnant girls were sent to the Florence Crittenden Home. The mentally ill had "nervous breakdowns" and disappeared for awhile. When Ray, my eighth grade classmate, began reading aloud a story about his alcoholic father, the teacher snatched it away and shoved it in her desk drawer.

In those few hours a week at the nursing home, I saw the hidden polio victims, their lips quivering as air was forced from their lungs, their eyes following me as I opened the window.

We called it polio, but the doctors labeled it infantile paralysis because it most often crippled and killed children under five. Polio was much more immediate to me than AIDS in the 80s. In 1952 alone, 350,000 Americans were infected.

My girlfriend's annual trip to summer camp was canceled because her family was afraid she'd catch the virus. My older cousin Kurt, the subject of my romantic fantasies, caught polio at college. He learned to walk again after months in bed.

Mom kept us kids away from the community swimming pool in Morse Park to protect us from polio carriers. How could I get polio, I wondered. Stepping into the locker room's murky footbath? Swimming too close to the poor kids who came from Edgewater and West High?

Mom called us inside on hot summer evenings when we rode our bicycles up and down the block, and the rain clouds boiled over the Rockies. Heat or overexertion might infect us with polio.

I was about ten when Father Jack and his wife, Rosie, moved next door. Jack had a thin face, with a dark shadow of beard under his skin like a stain of regret. He'd been infected with polio just after the Cincinnati Reds drafted him in the late 1940s. His legs were permanently paralyzed. Jack attended Episcopal seminary, graduated, and took a parish in our suburb. On Saturdays he stumped down his back steps on crutches, his shoes misshapen by iron braces. He called hello over the fence. Sometimes he clutched a baseball glove, dangling from fingers that also guided his crutches. As soon as my brother saw the glove, he galloped in the house to get his first baseman's mitt. Jack propped his crutches on the fence post, steadied himself against the rails, and played catch with an eight-year-old.

At night, I lay under the covers, looking at the slim pencil of light from under the door, and scared myself imagining I'd catch polio—an oddly stimulating terror like my earlier fears about the bogeyman and the H-bomb. I rehearsed the fear, playing it over, as if the thump of my heart, the movement of blood that whispered against the sheet, could keep me safe.

Then in 1955, news of the Salk vaccine hit our town. I devoured the news accounts, partly because scientists had won such a great victory over disease, but mostly because school was canceled for a day. Everyone was to get immunized. Mom drove us to the county health clinic in Golden. The courthouse basement rocked with noise, air thick with the smell of boys' sweaty socks. The line of youngsters zigzagged through the offices and coiled down the hall, past display cases filled with fly-spotted historic photographs, past the Motor Vehicle office where I would take the written driver's test when I turned sixteen.

Grade school kids raced the corridors, climbed the marble stairs, yelled over the banister. Pre-schoolers wailed from behind the privacy screens at the nurses' station.

I gossiped with my friends as I stood in line, about how many petticoats I wore under my circle skirt and which high school boy my classmate Sallie Bumpus had kissed behind the stands at the football game.

Late that afternoon, the county nurse rubbed an alcohol-soaked cotton ball on my arm. She slipped a thin needle into my skin. I turned away, too squeamish to watch as the vaccine—stuff that could save my life—slid into my vein.

I never received a polio shot again. Within a year or two, Frances Sabin's oral vaccine replaced the Salk vaccine, and I got my immunization from the school nurse who popped a saturated sugar cube in my mouth. Polio cases in the US dropped eighty percent. Jack and Rosie moved to California. Portable respirators unchained thousands of paraplegics from their iron lungs. The nursing home was torn down to build a shopping center.

In 1962, I visited the courthouse again with my

boyfriend. It was Saturday. The halls were dark and quiet. I was three months pregnant, a little queasy from the odor of oil left by the janitor's mop.

The county clerk bustled up to meet us, keys rattling as she unlocked her office. When we slipped her a $5 bribe, she gave us a license so we could get married that night. I didn't give polio a thought.

Anne Da Vigo is a novelist, journalist and public relations professional. Her thriller, Bakersfield Boys Club, *inspired by a series of real-life California murders, was a finalist in the Killer Nashville contest and received an honorable mention in the* Writers Digest *Self Published Book competition.*

Lost Hills
by Charles Bonneau

Part Three

Monday, July 14, 1919

No one I knew called it Bastille Day, though that
is what the Americans called it. To us it was simply the
Fourteenth of July, the day of national celebration, like the
Fourth of July.

To watch the parade, we had to get started early,
before heat descended on the city. So, by seven in the
morning everyone was out on Baker Street in their best
clothes, carrying flags. Papa pushed my wheelchair from
Humboldt down to Baker, then up to the corner, across the
street from the Carnegie Library.

In our little town, there was a July 14 parade every
year. This year, the marchers were gathered five blocks
north, at the corner of Baker and Bernard Street. They
were led by the mayor's car, who was joined by Monsieur
Bernard, the land developer. Following them was the
big float, decorated with red, white, and blue bunting
and portraits of Wilson, Lloyd George, and Clemenceau.
Nineteen-nineteen was special; it was the first French
national day parade since the Armistice. It was the victory
parade for the veterans, for those who had finally made
their way back home, and for those who did not.

Lady Liberty, a local girl, rode the float. She was a

fine choice that year, a striking brunette, Louise Verdier. She wore the traditional red Phrygian cap and a Grecian robe draped gracefully off one shoulder.

But the parade didn't start on time that morning. Louis Paquette's big Packard truck pulled the float to the assembly area. But when everyone was ready to march, the motor wouldn't start, for want of proper current through the ignition coil.

After much cursing and grunting the men gave up and borrowed horses from the Borel stable. Uncle Joe, carefully dressed in his army uniform by Tante Louise, was enlisted to lead the horses to the parade route.

The Percherons were great draft animals, gigantic and powerful, and gentle under Uncle Joe's hand. There was another delay to straighten out the harness and get the horses hitched to the float.

While we waited, Papa drifted off to smoke a cigar with his friends. The ladies of our neighborhood soon crossed the street, retreating to shade on the west side of the library. And, of course, Maman pushed me along. The women sat in a circle on the grass, each with her long dress spread out around her, each lady floating in her own pool of pastel fabric. Each lady wore a flowered hat tilted just so, each hat larger than the other.

These *belle époque* hats had come from Paris years before, in enormous cylindrical boxes two-thirds of a meter in diameter. They'd crossed the Atlantic to Panama with their owners, and crossed the Isthmus on the railroad, passing the abandoned machinery left by the DeLesseps enterprise, and the great heaps of soil moved by Old André and his companions before the yellow fever struck. Then they boarded the Pacific coast steamships which made their way up the long Mexican coast and finally to California.

Later, during the war, the government depopulated the Parisian workshops of the silk flower *artisanes*. The seamstresses went off to the munitions factories, measuring gunpowder into 75 mm casings and crimping firing caps into 8 mm *cartouches*. The days of the great headdresses never returned.

No more silk-flowered hats, alas. Nowadays, the war over, young girls of the nightlife in Paris paraded in tight-fitting caps, bobbed hair and short skirts, and danced to saxophone music. Ladies no longer promenaded the *corniche* displaying their giant floral artworks.

But what did we know of life in Europe, in the big city? To us life went on as always, our world frozen in amber. Each year, each lady still dusted off her huge silken headdress, for the *fête nationale* parade.

To pass the time while the parade was delayed, someone had the excellent idea that each lady should share the story of how she first met her husband or lover.

There were some amusing stories. One lady said that she first spotted her man silhouetted against the sky as he worked on a roof.

One woman was working as a maid when she took delivery of a dozen roses for her mistress, and fell in love with the delivery boy on the spot. One was cast in a play opposite the fellow who would soon ask her to marry him.

But the best story was told by Lucille Villeneuve's niece Irene, who was introduced to the ladies that day. Irene had evidently been staying somewhere outside of town, towards Arvin. Yet no one seemed to know her.

Irene was an attractive woman of uncertain age. She seemed young but oddly so, as if she had been away in a fairytale world, and had grown older without aging. There were telltale wrinkles around her eyes and streaks of grey hair, but her cheeks were smooth, and her full lips revealed gleaming white teeth.

"Well," she said, "I can tell you very well about that day. It was not long after I arrived here in Kern County.

"You all know the Caillard Ranch on Greenhorn Mountain." Everyone nodded and murmured. "I first arrived off the steamer in San Francisco to join my sisters. There was little employment, then I learned that I could sign on for work in a far-off place, down the Valley. I thought, why not? I was directed to the railway station in Oakland and given a ticket.

"What a trip that was! One day I was next to the Bay, on a foggy coast like Normandy. The next day I descended from the rail car and stood in a land," she paused to search for the right word, "in a land that some would say lacks charm."

The ladies laughed. "Well said! *Quel bon mot!*"

"I stayed here in town for a bit, then I was sent up the mountain with two other girls to look after the Caillard Ranch over the winter.

"What hard work! But when you're young you don't think about it, all the wood chopping and laundry. The long snowy days were spent cleaning and sewing.

"Then came the rains and mud everywhere. Finally, spring arrived. The old man told us that the first pack train was on its way down from Tehachapi.

"We heard them in the morning from far off, winding down the mountain trail through the forest. The men sang an old song, you may know it, the one about the daughter of the port commander of Nantes. Her father guarded her jealously, until a young adventurer came to steal her away. They sang in a round, so that the mules in the rear would know to keep up, and any a bear in the path ahead would be warned to get out of the way."

The ladies on the grass murmured among themselves,

recognizing the drudgery of the work and song of the men of the pack train.

"I worked in the kitchen, stoking the stove to feed the pack train crew. I whipped up the first batch of crêpe batter in a big ceramic bowl, waiting for the stove to heat up before taking the pans down from the ceiling and bringing the cooking oil up from the cool space under the floor. Then the song came echoing down the mountain, in a round as I said, with a beautiful lead voice.

"Soon they arrived in front of the ranch house. From inside, I listened as the men unharnessed the mules near the house and threw the harness and saddles on the porch and hauled the big bags of feed to the stable. I listened to one voice among them, a voice so sweet, such a good singing voice, so amusing and yet so strong. I stood inside the front door and smoothed my apron.

"Gabrielle came in from the back of the house with an armload of firewood. 'Aren't you going out to meet the young men?' she teased. 'No,' I said, 'I will wait here awhile and listen to the voice of the man I am to marry.'

"So that is my story." Irene smiled shyly. The women oohed and ahhed, and murmured in approval.

"But that is such a charming tale," my mother said as she leaned forward with intense curiosity. "I don't know your husband. Is he here?" Over Maman's shoulder I saw Tante Louise enter the ladies' circle. Tante Louise was ramrod straight, dressed as always in funereal black, with a stern expression even harsher than usual.

"Jules?" said Irene. "He's just down the street. He'll be delighted to meet you." Her aunt leaned over and whispered in Irene's ear. "But Lucille tells me he is occupied right now. Perhaps another time." Her gaze wandered away, and her lips moved wordlessly.

Up the street the crowd cheered as the parade finally

moved forward.

At the same moment Tante Louise leaned over and hissed at my mother. "Marie, come with me." Maman rose obediently. Back by my chair, Tante Louise was shaking with anger. "You should be ashamed; the boy should never be exposed to that woman."

Maman was bewildered. "But why? She seems nice enough, *assez gentille*."

"Didn't you know? *Elle est folle*, she is a madwoman. She is only in town because her aunt is taking her to Napa." "Napa" meant only one thing, the state mental hospital where insane people disappeared forever.

"That is terrible! But how would I know? I've never met her."

"You should know of her. She is the one who our brother fell in love with all these years ago, before you came here. But she married another man who became a soldier and was lost with the rest of them in 1917. You knew his parents, I believe."

"The Marinées? Our friends who sadly died? Ah *mon dieu*. How tragic. So that woman is why our Joseph is the way he is. That and the war." My mother was ready to weep.

We were back on the sidewalk in front of the library. The mayor's car had just gone by at the head of the parade. We dashed across the street, Maman pushing the wheelchair as it bumped over the curb. There we stood in front of the hardware store under the red, white, and blue bunting, in the morning glare.

There was Uncle Joe, leading the float horses with his good arm. Joe had a way with the animals, but the Percherons weren't used to parade duty. One would pause as the other paced forward.

Meanwhile, Lady Liberty clung gamely to her perch, holding the torch with one hand and clutching her half-draped Grecian robe over her half-exposed left breast with the other, as the float jerked and jiggled. The crowd was enthralled, as much by the jiggles as the jerks.

Across the street next to the library, Irene was standing now, in the crowd of cheering women, looking off into nowhere. Her lips soundlessly repeated something, perhaps the words of the story that the ladies had found so enchanting. She still had the eternal youthful beauty of the half-departed.

In his sky-blue uniform with his ribbons and his great white moustache, Uncle Joe was visibly proud. By some infernal coincidence, he never looked toward the library. He was easily distracted when we clapped and shouted. *"Vive la Republique!"* *"Vive les poilus!"* He never saw Irene, never knew she was there. And she never looked in his direction.

The float was followed by the veterans' band, wheezing out the *Marseillaise*. The band was missing most of the brass section, never to return. Two flutes were in wheelchairs, and the bass drummer was missing an arm.

Papa finally rejoined us. Then came the veterans, marching in blue ranks, and the American honor guard in khaki, then the Boy Scouts, then another band, from the downtown high school. My mother and Tante Louise began to relax. Irene and her aunt had disappeared. It was time for the parents to push me home and prepare the house for an afternoon of wine and fiddle playing and dancing.

The parade began to disband just beyond the train station. Men flocked to help Lady Liberty dismount from the float.

The city sanitation sweeper came down the empty street, pushing his barrow between the streetcar tracks and cleaning up after the horses and the people.

I felt a cold shiver of guilt and remorse, despite the blazing heat. "You weren't fair to your uncle today." It was the Voice, behind me again. I twisted in my chair but of course there was nothing to see.

"How could I know that? The adults all thought it was better this way."

"Yes, but sometimes you know better than they do."

"It's too late now, and anyway how do I know better than the adults?"

"Your uncle has a right to know what has happened to the woman he loved, even if it breaks his heart. You will learn about love later. But you already know right from wrong." And then the Voice was gone.

Maman's voice broke into my thoughts. "What are you muttering? People will think you've lost your mind, like that unfortunate young woman."

"Nothing mother, I was reciting my lessons to myself."

"You should be more discreet."

"Yes, Maman." We left ahead of the lonely street sweeper, toiling in the blazing sun.

―――――――――――――――

Charles Bonneau passes his time in Davis, California, with his wife Dottie and numerous offspring. He continues to work past his prime, as an attorney in the courts of appeal. He has an on-going interest in French history and culture.

The Doe
by Scott Evans

He shook when he heard the explosion outside. Half asleep, he climbed out of bed and stepped into the hallway. It was empty. He looked down the staircase. The radio in the kitchen played a soft old song, like one his mother had listened to. He walked down the stairs slowly. Dishes piled in the sink. The smell of burnt toast. His father was outside somewhere. Sam stepped out of the kitchen door into the dark. The shop light threw a design of squares on the ground from the windows. He saw the floodlight go on across the road, Mr. Ramsey worried about the noise. Barefoot, Sam walked across the cold, wet ground to the shop and went inside. He saw the body. His father lay on his back, part of his shirt collar gone, his face shoveled out. Sam's single-barrel shotgun, locked in the vice of the workbench, pointed over the body. The light was on. A car rushed down the road but did not stop. Sam went over. It didn't look like his father's face.

Ramsey's voice outside made Sam turn around. The shop door was open. Ramsey was with his boy walking to the front of the house. Mr. Ramsey would knock politely at the front door and wait. He'd go inside reluctantly and look around for Sam and his dad, calling out their names. It would be a while before he thought to come out back. Sam had a few minutes. He sat down next to his father, his back to what was left of his head, and wondered why his dad had used his shotgun. It was shorter, so it was easier to reach the trigger, he guessed, if you're standing in front of it....

The first time Sam had carried a rifle on a hunting trip with his father was two years ago when he was twelve, and he was frightened that morning before light that he would have an accident and shoot his father or his brother or his uncle, so he had done exactly what his old man had said and sat rigidly still with his back against a tree trunk facing south with a view down the sloping hill across the gully to the ridge where the sun was supposed to come from. He held a Winchester .32 Special between his legs and waited, the taste of milk-coffee souring his mouth, the chill of the morning digging into the seat of his pants and stinging his earlobes and nose. He listened to the noiseless forest and tried to keep his breath quiet, and hoped with every heartbeat that a buck would bound his way. He knew his father was waiting similarly only twenty-five yards to the east, holding his Remington .256 across his lap. He could picture the tense way his father held the rifle strap twisted around one arm, his other hand around the grip and his finger just away from the trigger. He could picture his father in the dark, all the sounds that he himself couldn't yet hear coming alive for his father. His brother was even farther east on the slope with his prized .30/30, probably slurping coffee, his rifle on the ground beside him. His uncle sat thirty yards to his west. Their plan was to wait for sunrise, and after an hour, on the whistle command from his father, to walk down and fan out to flush a buck for one of them. A stream ran at the bottom of the gully. On its banks, during their scouting trip, they had noticed deer spoor and fresh buck tracks in the mud, signs that told his father the habit of the deer was to come from the grassy knoll to the west down to the stream to water in the morning, then ascend the ridge where they were and tread east to an afternoon spot for grazing among the cover of manzanita and young oak.

The sound of a squirrel clucking above awoke Sam. He had drifted to sleep for just a minute but was safe because dawn had not yet begun. The ridge had come alive with scattered noises, intermittent sounds of dry tree branches and leaves under weight of smaller animals.

Sam awoke the second time with the sun on his face. Fear shot through him when he knew he had slept and not responded to his father's signal. Then a shot rang out from below, and he pushed himself to his feet, rifle in hand and heard another shot. He couldn't place the rifle exactly, but thought it might be the loud report of his uncle's .308, so he readied himself and began down the ridge. He swung around to his right when he saw the deer, slinging his rifle up to match the sights against the wide neck, and fired, cocked and fired, and the doe dropped.

Sam knew what he had done almost before he pulled the trigger on the second shot, but there was no way to retrieve the lead once it had left the shell. That had been his feeling, like trying to catch a canary escaping from a cage, an impulse to reach out and grab the thing in flight. It was a clean shot through the base of the skull. At least there was that much, the knowledge that the doe had not suffered. Sam dropped his rifle beside the body and kneeled down, watching fleas and ticks crawl toward the wound. Her tongue hung out and her eyes were wide with shock.

Brian was the first to reach him. Sam had stopped crying by then and was just sitting near the doe, waiting.

"Dad will shit when he sees," Brian said. "He will absolutely shit! You're dead, boy. Your hunting days are over."

"Shut up!"

"Why didn't you look?"

"I thought I saw a rack."

"Dad is going to shit."

"Shut up!"

His uncle came up next. He didn't say a word. He looked down at the doe for a few minutes. Then he lit his pipe and smiled. "You shot the horns right off that buck, boy," he said and laughed.

"I'm sorry."

"You'll be a helluva lot sorrier when your old man sees her."

Sam just sat and waited. He could hear his father's footsteps crushing the dry leaves from down below.

"Young Sam got himself about seventy pounds of venison," his uncle called. All of them knew what that meant. He could hear his father still coming up the side of the ridge.

He wanted to cry but knew he shouldn't. He stood up with his rifle. Brian moved away. He could see his father now looking up at him as he climbed, the orange vest and hat standing out against the dark browns of Autumn.

"How'd that happen?" his father finally asked after staring down at the deer.

"I don't know," he said.

His father's hand came hard against the side of his head.

"You're the only one who does know, Sam."

"I didn't walk down with the rest of you. I stayed up here."

"I knew you had. How come?"

"I fell asleep."

"Oh, Jesus!" Brian laughed.

His father turned around. "You shut up." He looked

back to Sam.

"When I woke up, I heard shots and started down. The doe jumped, and I fired on her."

"It was a good, clean shot, Ed," his uncle said.

"There was nothing wrong with the boy's aim," his father said.

His father reached over and took Sam's rifle. "You carry your doe, son. We'll dress her down, of course, and use her meat. Just hope a game warden doesn't wander into camp."

Sam looked his father in the eyes. His father was a dark, large man whose eyes were as clear and stern as two freshly minted dimes, whose day-old beard was as black as charcoal. The lines of his face had been creased by the constant grimace his work as a logger demanded. In his father's face Sam saw the disappointment and disgust that made his own gut fill with acid. All he could do now to make up for the killing of the doe was to act the best way he could, carry out his father's instructions as well as he knew how to during the remainder of the hunting trip. If he could hold onto everything and be his best, he thought there might be a chance for him to get his rifle back and finish the hunting trip with some reward.

"Should we gut her out here to lighten Sam's load, Ed?"

"We'll want to hunt this area again tomorrow. I don't want the smell disturb-ing the run of those deer."

Sam bent down and pulled the legs of the doe together. They hadn't gone stiff yet. Sam tugged the body toward a rise of ground and tried to lift it, dropping down to one knee as he had seen his father do when trying to pick up a buck. He struggled to get the seventy pounds onto his shoulders, holding onto the legs just above the hooves. The legs still bent, the muscles still flexible in his grip, and she dropped back down, a gush of air sounding through the watery throat. Finally, Brian came over and helped him get the doe up on his shoulders, and he fixed the doe in his hands as securely as he could and started back up toward their camp. He took the lead, knowing his father and his uncle and his older brother were watching. He made sure of his footing with each step. Whenever he came to a soft bit of soil, he tested it before putting all his weight down. He knew he didn't want to fall.

The belly of the doe against the back of his neck felt warm and disturbing, like hot jelly inside a skin sack. He could feel the ticks and fleas climb into his hair and down inside his shirt. Sometimes when his feet came down hard, a gush of air would cause the body to cough or hiss as if she were still alive. He felt himself break out with sweat. The way he carried the doe, high up on his shoulders, bent over under the weight, the loose head wobbled as he walked up the ridge and sometimes the snout would brush against the side of his face. Blood was dripping from the wound behind the skull, dripping on the back of his boots, probably. He would have to dress down the deer himself.

He knew that much. He had watched it done enough, and had reached inside enough to know how, and he had severed the skin from the muscle enough to know how to work the knife like a saw, taking little slices at the membrane that secured the skin to the body. He would have to wipe her down and bury the guts deep and wash himself and his clothing. He knew how much trouble they would be in if a game warden came to inspect their camp. He knew all about what he had done and reviewed all of it in his mind as he walked back. He didn't pretend to be tired or sick and held everything together inside.

When he mounted the top of the ridge, he stopped and waited, and, standing above the others with the doe on his shoulders looking down at the others climbing, he felt satisfied and relieved. He knew the worst was over and he felt good that he could do the retribution that was required. Most boys my age can't fire a rifle worth a damn, and don't know how to take care of a mistake when they've made one. I can do this. I can take care of it by myself. It's not as bad as I thought. I could carry this deer forever if I had to.

"I was only over anxious, dad," he said aloud. His father came up the hill and stood in front of him. There was no meanness left in his eyes.

"What was your mistake, son. Tell me."

Sam thought back over it, and didn't let it sicken him. He thought about it the way he would a school problem, the way he knew his father would want him to, the way a man chooses a tree to fell and the angle just as his father had described.

"Well, two things. I didn't keep myself awake, and I didn't check out my game properly. I didn't make sure of what I was shooting at."

"Maybe I made a mistake, too," his father said. "Maybe it's a mistake to think that a twelve-year-old boy is old enough to hunt like a man."

Sam looked down. He felt weak, suddenly.

"Do you think I made a mistake, Sam?"

Sam waited until he could speak without the sound of crying in his throat.

"No, sir. I think I am old enough now."

"We'll talk about it again later, and I'll decide then."

"Yes, sir."

His uncle and Brian had walked on ahead. His father went on. Sam was in the rear, now. He let himself cry only a little on the rest of the way back. The wet nose of the doe slapped him in the face as he tried to keep up.

He could only look down. It was a strain to look ahead, and impossible to look up at the sky. He was sweating good, now, the sun high enough in the morning to bring heat.

The horrible thing his father had to do once they were in camp was take the hammer they used to drive in the tent poles and smash the skull of the doe with several blows so no one could tell if there had been a rack or not, and he did it before Sam had dressed it down, before he had even taken the hacksaw and cut off the head, so that while Sam worked on her, he would always have to look at the pulpy head. He sawed off the legs first at the place just after the bones joined so he could still hang her by the hind legs.

Once they had her up, hanging her first by the neck, his father came over and cut the skin of her lower belly just as if it had been a buck and the penis and testicles had to be removed. Then Sam sliced the belly open and gutted her, reaching up with his hands and pulling the stomach and intestines out and severing them from inside with the knife.

Next he went up inside the abdominal wall as his uncle instructed and felt for the trachea and severed it from inside, and they pulled out the lungs and heart. His father saved the heart. Then Sam took her down and cut off the head and re-hung her by her hind legs, slipping a bar of wood through the intersection of bone and tendon on each leg and tugging her high by pulling the rope through the pulley on the tree limb above. Brian helped hold her up until Sam could get the rope tied off. Then he took the knife and began skinning her. None of it affected Sam. He had watched his father do it and his uncle and other men several times each season since he was old enough to recall. It was nearly the same procedure he followed with all game, and so there was nothing horrible or grotesque about it, except that it was a female. He felt sorry for her while he worked and wished he had not been overly anxious to shoot his deer. He wished with all his might that she was still living, and he hoped that her fawns—if she had any—were old enough to be on their own, and he felt relieved when he checked her nipples and saw that they were dry.

Everything was in a cardboard box except the heart and liver and head, and after Sam had wiped down the glistening muscle with a damp rag torn from an old sheet and tied a deer bag over her, he took the box and head and shovel and hiked far enough from camp to bury it all. He dug a hole wide and deep. He had not eaten yet that day and was hungry and could smell the bacon from the camp. It took him a long time to dig the hole. All around him the manzanita and tall trees seemed to move with sunlight. He constantly checked to see if someone watched, but there was no one except his family back in the camp.

He knew the smell had probably attracted some animals already, and knew he would have to dig a hole at least four feet deep or they would be awakened in the night. He finally took his jacket off before filling in the hole. The dirt was easy enough to dig in, rich and wet, giving up the odor of the forest.

Whenever he had come upon a stone, he removed it to use on top of the mound. Working slower, he filled in the grave and finished it by setting stones over it. The fleas had bitten the skin under his arms and around his waist. His pants were on tight enough to keep them out. He looked at his jacket while he walked back to camp. Blood stained the shoulders and one sleeve, and he picked off any ticks or fleas he found.

At the camp things seemed clean to him. The deer

was taken care of. His uncle was cooking at the fire and looked up, smiling with the pipe clamped between his teeth. The smoke from the fire and from his uncle's pipe both curled away in the same direction. Brian and his father were eating. The deer was hanging from a tree just beyond his uncle's jeep. He knew he would have to re-hang her farther from camp, higher up so nothing could get at her. But he could do that later. He had to eat something and get himself cleaned up.

"You better wash yourself," Brian said.

"He can eat first," his uncle said.

"He stinks, and he's got blood dried all over his ugly mug."

Uncle Fred splashed hot grease toward Brian. "Let him eat, sissy."

"Is it okay to, Pa?"

"Sure, Sam. Eat fast, though, and go wash."

Uncle Fred handed him a plate of beans cooked in bacon grease with some eggs scrambled on top and a slice of bacon on the side of the plate. Brian tossed two slices of white bread on his plate and handed him a fork.

"Brian made some of that lemonade you like."

He took a paper cup and held it out for his father to fill. Then he sat down in the dirt near the fire and ate as quickly as he could, washing down the mouthfuls with lemon-ade that was too weak. While he ate, his father went to their tent and gathered another pair of pants and a tee-shirt for him. He wrapped the clothes around a bar of soap with a towel, then went back and finished his breakfast. When Sam and his father were done, they walked down the ridge to the stream together, walking far downstream so the soap suds would not spoil their game's drinking water or their own. Sam stripped, put all his clothes in the water, and weighted them down with two large stones.

"They bit all the hell over you, boy. Christ almighty."

Sam found a tick dug in under his arm and twisted it free. His father struck a match, blew it out and held it to a tick on his back. Sam looked carefully down his arms, then on his chest and stomach and groin, and felt inside his legs where he couldn't look. He felt his father untwist one on his back and hold a match to another one down on his waist.

He checked down his legs and looked at his feet. There were several red welts where the fleas had bitten him. They didn't hurt much and the fleas seemed gone.

Sam stepped into the icy water and splashed himself shaking and soaping his legs.

"You're lucky you don't have much hair around your dingus yet or else they'd be all in there."

Sam laughed and washed himself. He climbed out of the water after washing up to his waist. The chill made his flesh as bumpy as a plucked chicken. He pulled on his pants and kneeled down by the water.

"Get your hair good and wet, Sam."

He dunked his whole head in the water and could feel the bottom grit on his scalp as he shampooed the soap into his hair. Sam took the towel from his father again and dried his hair as hard as he could. He hung the towel over his shoulder while his father checked his scalp for ticks and fleas.

"Looks okay," he said, and Sam washed his face and arms and shoulders and chest. He dried himself off quickly and shivered and pulled on the clean tee-shirt his father had. He kept the towel wrapped around his neck, picked up his boots and started to get his other clothes that had been weighted down in the stream the whole time he'd been washing up.

"Leave them for a while, Sam. You and Brian can

walk down later this afternoon."

"Yes, sir."

They started back up the trail, Sam shivering from the water and the fall air. Then they stopped while his father took off his heavy plaid shirt and handed it to Sam. Sam buttoned it up with numb hands. He looked at his father's face. His father stayed quiet, then whispered, "Hold it."

They stood still. He could hear it, too, the sound of something stepping cautiously across dried leaves. He glanced at his father. His father was searching the hillside up ahead in the direction of the noise. The manzanita stood as tall as Sam and provided good cover.

His father stepped ahead slowly, looking down to avoid the small dry leaves that had already fallen from the bushes. Sam followed him as carefully as he could, trying to keep his bare feet on the dirt. He followed slowly along the path and cut back in toward the stream with his father. They stopped on the path and listened. He heard only the distant sound of trees creaking in the breeze, but no near sound. Then they could both hear each small footstep again, one, then the other, then a pause and the hind feet. It was a tense cautious sound that made Sam nervous. He couldn't tell how far away it was. They just stood and listened until it stopped. Then Sam's father cut down closer to the stream, and he followed.

The brush was clear from the banks of the stream, and only the dry weed covered the dirt, some rocks and moss and low viny poison oak. Sam looked upstream and was shocked when he saw the huge rack on the buck facing them twenty-five yards away. The buck was at the water's edge, head dropped, but up from the water looking straight at them. He did not move for a long time. Sam and his father only looked and stayed very still. It was a good sized buck, one of the largest Sam had ever seen. He tried to keep his breathing even. Finally, the buck lowered his head to the water and drank as though he knew Sam and his father did not have rifles. He lapped up the cold water for a long while, alone, only the noise of the water sheeting over the rocks disturbing the silence. Sam could see how beautiful he was, his skin clean of scars, nicely colored and even.

The buck drank delicately from the stream. Sam counted five points on one side and four on the other. He thought the spread might be a foot and a half or better. He thought the buck would dress down to more than twice the weight of the doe.

Then he thought about the doe again, and felt bad inside that he had shot her. When he was younger, his uncle had told him stories about the ghosts of the Pomo Indians watching over the hunting of deer. He had described the dance of the deer which the Pomos danced the night before a hunt. It was a kind of dance that both asked forgiveness and asked that the female deer be fertile to provide food. His uncle had told him that the Pomos never disgraced their spirits by asking for help with their hunting, but instead always asked that the deer be protected. Sam wondered if any of it were true....

Now Sam Edwards was sitting with his back toward his father's body, thinking about the hunting trip when he heard Mr. Ramsey call out his father's name. They were headed toward the shop. He knew he should go out and warn them. It would be a bad sight for them. He knew he should stand up and step just outside and warn them, but he couldn't quite stand. He watched them pass through the darkness between the rear of the house and the front of the shop where the light from the open shop door angled out and slanted across the ground. He saw Ramsey and his son come into the light of the door and look at him, and he saw Mr. Ramsey's face, a weird grin of bewilderment at seeing Sam on the floor.

"What the hell, Sammy?" Ramsey said, his voice ringing. Then, "Oh, Christ, boy! Oh, Christ!"

"I'm okay," Sam heard himself say. "I'm okay."

He felt himself stand and watch Ramsey put his hand across his son's eyes and push his son outside, back, into the darkness.

"I'm okay," Sam heard himself say again. "It's my dad. He had an accident."

Sam watched Ramsey go over to the body and put his hand down flat on his chest. His father's legs were splayed oddly, the feet turned all the way to the ground, all the muscle tone gone. Sam could see all of it now, the spray of blood and disintegrated skin on the wall, the shredded shirt collar, the odd way one arm was limp underneath the body, the glint of gold light from the wristband of his father's watch on the other arm, the oily-looking damp area beyond the head, the dust on the floorboards.

Sam watched Ramsey's head swivel from side to side, watched him turn and face the shotgun mounted in the vice on the workbench and nod. Ramsey stood and looked back down at the body.

"What happened, Sammy?"

"I think he had an accident."

Ramsey looked at him in an odd way.

"Are you alright?"

"I think so. Maybe I should walk around."

Sam could see Ramsey's boy standing off in the dark. Mr. Ramsey nudged Sam, and he walked toward the house. Ramsey called to his son. He said something Sam could not hear. Sam felt his heart racing. His heart was trying to bounce free of his chest. He reached up to his throat to feel the throb in the soft skin under his jaw. He tried to turn around to tell Mr. Ramsey.

Sam couldn't move when he came to. He could hear voices, but he couldn't see. Then he felt the stinging in his arms and legs, and then his temples began to pound and he could open his eyes. He tried to move, but he couldn't. His skin seemed stung by thin needles.

It was hot. He knew he was sweating. He couldn't see, although he knew his eyes were open. Then he saw what looked like the white torn edge of black paper, a thick ribbon of lightness, like a crack in black stone that had caught a dull light. He could see that there were clouds overhead, moonlight painting their edges. He couldn't see the moon, but he knew it must be bright to light up the edges of the clouds. Then he heard a voice and he saw Mr. Ramsey's face over him, dark in shadow, glasses shiny with blackness.

"We're going to carry you."

Sam tried to stand. He saw Mrs. Ramsey at his feet.

"No," he said. "Let me lay here."

"Are you hurt, Sammy," the woman asked.

"No, just let me lay here."

He shut his eyes and could feel the needles in his arms and legs turn cold.

Suddenly, the memory flowed through him, and he began to cry. He cried heavily with spasms that made it hard to breathe, and then he stopped. He didn't have to cry any longer. He thought about his father. He could sit up, but felt weak.

Mr. Ramsey put his hand on Sam's shoulder. They helped him stand and walk into the house. They went into the living room and Sam lay down on the couch.

He put his arm over his eyes in the light. He heard

Mr. Ramsey dial the phone. He listened to Mr. Ramsey talk to the police. He heard Ramsey say, "A man shot himself."

"Sammy? Sammy?" Mrs. Ramsey said.

She's a skinny woman, Sam thought. How could she carry me? Sam could see her face in his mind, her reddish complexion, the brown glasses like cat eyes making her face look clownish.

In his mind, he could see the buck again, the way it dipped its head down into the water, the way the rack followed the motions of the head, rigidly and erect, the way the flesh quivered on the hind quarter to shake off flies, the way the legs seemed perfect and sculptured, no waste of muscle or bone. He thought about shivering in the cold autumn air with his father watching the animal with pleasure and envy, enjoying every second they were allowed to look at him. It was a true privilege. Sam had not realized what a privilege it had been for both of them. You have to earn a privilege like that, he thought.

The buck finally stopped drinking and backed up nervously on the bank. The stream was wide and swift, but in one leap that caught Sam off guard, the buck made the jump from one bank to the other and trotted up the other side of the gully, disappearing inside the cover of the trees.

A thousand moments flooded his mind about the hunting trip. He knew he would have to sort all of it out, all the memories like photos he had inherited which were more than photos, all of them building to something. He felt certain he could work through all of it and find out something he needed to know.

He had a clear picture of his father standing with uncle Fred in camp an evening later, passing a bottle of Jack Daniels whiskey back and forth, pouring gulp sized portions in their mess cups. He had a clear picture of his father cutting the hindquarter from the doe later for a large dinner meal. There was a picture of his uncle slicing onions and carrots into a pot next to his father cleaning a rifle. He remembered wondering how they could get along so well when he and Brian hated each other so much. He recalled the misery he felt during the four days of the hunting trip that he was not allowed to hunt.

On the last day, Sam's father handed his rifle back in the afternoon and told him he could hunt with them that evening. They would leave the next morning. Sam wanted to hunt that evening with all his might. He cleaned his rifle and put all his gear in order.

The four of them had used both hind-quarters from the doe by then, and no one had shot a buck yet. It seemed as though Sam had jinxed the trip, and he wanted to prove to them he hadn't.

The evening plan was to hike west from camp to the grassy knoll and sweep down the other side of the ridge downstream as far as they could before sundown. They would want enough time to hunt back-tracking before dark, so they could only walk for an hour or so downstream. At six o'clock, they started out.

They walked together on a path from camp to the knoll, then spread out about thirty yards apart along the side of the ridge to make their sweep. Sam was nearest the stream. He liked having the sound of the rushing water near him to drown out the footsteps.

He focused intently ahead, holding his rifle high vertically. He wanted to be able to drop his sights in a second. He didn't look down, although he nearly tripped several times on the round stones abundant by the stream. He felt his boots turn heavily over the stones, the leather pressing in on his ankles, but he kept his eyes trained ahead. He wanted to train his sights on a deer and be able to recognize it as buck or doe as quickly as physically possible. It was as if at any moment an enormous spring would fly at him, his own foot triggering its release. From time to time, he looked up the ridge and saw his father walking far up alongside between the trees. The low red sun behind them darkened the ridge with shadows stretched to their limits.

With the low shadows laying down from the trees and bushes, merging, and with the sense of night coming and the smell of the leaves that was the smell of autumn, Sam felt everything ending. The trip was ending, and his strange feeling of newness was ending. While he stepped carefully, intently ahead, he was aware of the sunlight and shadow and of his father and of the sound of the water and the smell of the decaying dry leaves in the cool air. He felt the coolness of the smooth wood of his gunstock. He could feel his legs straining, the fibers of muscles being pulled whenever his foot twisted over the top of a round stone. He could feel the firmness of the dry clay underfoot, the way it felt hollow far down.

The buck was not with the doe that leaped from the cover of a manzanita bush ahead and bounded up the ridge in front of all of them. He had raised his rifle, sighted on her but had not fired, and with a glance, he watched his father sight on her, too. He tensed up and waited. In the time it took for the branches to crack on the brush, the fawn sprang out in another direction and ran scared between Sam and his father. He waited, half expecting to hear a shot from his brother or his uncle. The woods were silent. Only the water beside him splashed between stones. Then he heard his father start again. He waited until his father had a lead of a few yards and then stepped ahead slowly.

He concentrated on the brush ahead, expecting the

buck to come out, but soon he was in the same brush and there was nothing. He stopped and looked around. There was no sign of another deer. He squinted to look through the branches of other manzanita bushes around him to see some trace of hide. There was nothing.

They made the sweep farther down until the shadows lost edges, and Sam started up the ridge, walking easily up the lesser incline.

"I thought sure there'd be a buck," he told his father.

"I thought there might be, too."

"You think he was there all the time, dad? You think he got past us?"

"Maybe. They're smart bastards."

"I thought we might see that one again," he said. They had started up together and his father was smoking a Camel now.

"We'll never see him again, Sammy. I ain't sure we ever did."

"Sure we did. We looked at his tracks afterward."

His father sucked in hard on the small cigarette while they walked up. Uncle Fred was sitting waiting for them.

"This has been a helluva fun trip, Ed."

"I don't understand it," Sam's father said. Sam stayed quiet, thinking again that he had jinxed the trip.

His father gave Uncle Fred a Camel and lit it for him, and they started up toward Brian. It was getting darker. Sam thought they might have trouble finding their way back. They had walked too far down. He turned around to look down at the water. He couldn't hear it anymore, and all he could see of it was a dark ribbon laced behind all the trees and brush down at the end of the hill.

The shot made Sam jerk. It surprised them all. He looked at his father who was looking at Uncle Fred.

"I'll be damned!" his uncle said.

They stepped quickly up, climbing with their rifles in their hands, Sam in the lead.

When he found him, Brian was standing over the buck like the hunters they had seen in photographs of African safaris. He had his rifle at his side, one foot up on the shoulders of the buck, his right hand tucked Napoleon-style into his shirt. His head was tilted so far back it made his eyes look closed.

"You bastard!" Sam laughed. "You got him!"

"Dropped him with one shot, Sam, old bean!" Brian stayed in his stance while he spoke, assuming a mock-British accent.

Sam bent down over the buck's head.

"You ruined the trophy, but that's okay."

"So I split the rack! Who gives a rat's ass!"

Their father came up smiling with Uncle Fred.

Sam held onto that picture as long as he could, the picture of his father walking up in the dim light smiling, his weapon pointed safely down under his arm, Uncle Fred climbing behind him. Sam tried to keep that image from fading. It would have made a good picture, he thought. It was stupid having all the people around now, when all he wanted to do was think and remember. He knew he couldn't hold onto a picture like that for long. He knew something would ruin it.

The Sheriff's deputy was there. Sam sat up and said hello. He told the deputy that he heard the shot from his room and went down. The deputy is a young guy, he thought. He can't be much older than me.

"How old are you, sir?" he asked.

"I'm twenty," the deputy said, as if it was the most normal question he had ever heard. "How old are you, Sammy?"

"Fourteen."

The deputy grinned. "A lot happens in six years, Sam."

Sam thought about that for awhile. He looked at Mr. Ramsey looking at him. Where did Mrs. Ramsey go? he wondered. I guess people pretty much feel they can come and go in my house as they please now.

"Sammy?" the deputy said.

"Yes, sir?"

"You didn't shoot your father, did you?"

Sam looked at the deputy's face. He's serious, Sam thought. Sam thought he might laugh.

Then he thought if he started laughing, he might not be able to stop. It was the oddest feeling he had ever had, a feeling that he might laugh and not ever be able to stop.

"Sam's father has had cancer for quite some time, deputy. We all knew he was in pain lately." Mr. Ramsey's voice was steady and quiet, almost a whisper.

"It was a secret about the cancer," Sam told the deputy.

Sam got onto his feet. Both the deputy and Mr. Ramsey were a head or so taller than him. He measured himself off against them, and a funny thought went through his mind to fight them. He didn't like what the deputy had asked.

"How do you feel, son?" the deputy asked.

"Like I want a big drink of my dad's whiskey."

The deputy looked at Ramsey and they nodded. Who the hell are they to give me permission to drink in my own goddamn house?. He went into the kitchen and the both of them followed. He opened the cabinet and looked up.

"Want to hand the Jack Daniels down, sir."

"Sure, son."

Sam took off the top and swallowed enough to burn. He'd drunk it enough with buddies and even with his old man and uncle to know how to take it down slowly. He swallowed a little more and handed back the bottle.

"That'll make me feel better."

"It sure should," Mr. Ramsey said.

"What happens now?" Sam asked. "What should we do?"

The deputy put the bottle back on the shelf and closed the cabinet door quietly. He pulled the string for the light over the sink. Sam didn't like the place much since his mother had died. He hated the way it was always filthy.

"We put things in order, Sammy. We let the coroner look at your father and we take him to the mortuary and we decide where you're going to stay."

"And we pray, Sammy," Mr. Ramsey said. "We pray for your father."

Sam looked at Ramsey's eyes. They were watery behind his glasses.

"I'm not much of a prayer," he told them. "You know, I ought to call my brother. He's away at college. He ought to know. And I'd better call Uncle Fred."

"Does your uncle live nearby?" the deputy asked him.

"He lives over by the coast. He's got a small ranch south of Fort Bragg."

"He could be here in a couple of hours."

Sam went to the dark screen door. The shop light was still on, its yellow light spilling out across the ground through the wide doorway. He could feel the chilly air sweeping in through the screen. The night was quiet, no locusts or crickets humming, no wind and no cars on the road.

Then, far off, he heard the sound of something.

Moaning maybe. High-pitched whining. Perhaps it was a baby crying or a male cat screaming in a fight somewhere far off.

He'd hate to be way out there in the night. He'd hate to have to be a tomcat out there in a fight, screaming. The sound was like a cat, but too far away, under the huge canopy of clouds and darkness.

"Do you want to make that call, Sammy?" he heard one of the men ask. It was a funny thing to ask because just then he thought they were talking about the cry of the tomcat. Do I want to make that call? Then he knew what they meant, but still it was funny to him. He felt like calling out in the night, answering the cry of the frightened tomcat or the wail of the baby or the moan of the man who was way off in the darkness, but then he realized that the sound was nothing like he thought. It wasn't a human sound or a sound from an animal in distress. It was only the weird whine of a siren beating through the darkness toward him.

Preface to *Green Seasons*, a short story collection that includes "The Doe":

Back in 1985, my office mate at LSU & I made a trade: a duplicate copy he owned of Peter Buckley's *Ernest*, a volume containing numerous photographs of and by Hemingway, for an extra bound copy of my recently finished dissertation on the American short story sequence. I still use Buckley's book often when I teach Hemingway in my classes on the short story sequence, and I always thought that I came out better in that trade. Yet little did I know then that—twenty-five years later—my former office mate, Scott Evans, would bring those two streams of influence together in this collection, *Green Seasons*.

These stories chronicle the initiation of a young American male whose life experiences reveal—in a series of significant lessons—that in the context of the last half of the late twentieth century, the time our culture mythologizes as the idyllic seasons of one's youth is one of vulnerability, prone to tragedy and loss that teach the hard lessons of mortality. Yet these experiences also provide the means to grow and to learn to live in that world, by demonstrating the "grace under pressure" that Hemingway lauded in bullfighters and depicted in his code heroes.

There are clear allusions to Hemingway throughout *Green Seasons*, especially to "A Clean Well Lighted Place" in "The Rains" and to a number of stories in *In Our Time*, whose form Evans adapts for the collection. Like Nick Adams, Evans's recurrent protagonist Sam leaves the familiar and heads out into the world, though he already bears the burden of loss. Traveling north, to a landscape evocative of Hemingway's Michigan, he learns to survive on his own in a challenging world while wrestling with the ethical dilemmas posed by the Vietnam war for young men of draft age. The source of the emotional and psychological scars that his experiences in that war leave is dramatically withheld until the penultimate story, "Baptism," and the river on which Sam travels in the final story evokes Hemingway's classic "Big Two-Hearted River," in which Nick struggles to stop his thoughts, to keep control, and to live deliberately in the moment. *Green Seasons* also features clear stylistic echoes of the master of crisp short sentences & pared down prose, though in crucial moments the style and imagery are allowed rise to a more lyrical plateau. Other verbal echoes of Hemingway should provide pleasure for those who rank as his aficionados, as will the thematic and formal resonance with *In Our Time*, an early but seminal work in Hemingway's career. Though the chrono-logical time element provides a frame for *Green Seasons*, each story has decided closure; across the gaps between stories, however, character and imagery create cohesion, with recurrent references to blood providing the strongest and most dramatic thread.

Some publishers call the form that Evans is using in *Green Seasons* the "novel-in-stories," but such a label causes the reader to bring expectations to the work that interfere with accepting it on its own terms. Indeed, the stories that make up this work are chronological, yet they purposefully lack that causal spine and tight cohesion one expects in the novel, as well as the "what next?" feeling of a suspended plot that the reader experiences at the end of a novel's chapters. Perhaps our expectations and not the label are what need to be different, but other terms alert the reader better about the nature of the form and endow such volumes with a unique status among literary genres. While some reviewers simply call such works collections of "interrelated stories," the most accurate label is perhaps "short story sequence," which not only draws attention to the dramatic and emotional arc of the volume as a whole but also reminds us that each unit possesses the firm closure that we expect from the short story—one of its chief pleasures. Nonetheless, though each story is autonomous, together they are more than the sum of their parts, resonating meaningfully with each other.

To hazard some sort of definition, the short story sequence might be described as a volume of stories collected and organized by the author into an aesthetic whole, so that the reader successively realizes inter-relationships between autonomous stories, underlying/overarching patterns of organization and coherence, and thematic unity through a continual modification of his/her perceptions as the volume is read sequentially. Yet short story sequences vary markedly: some derive their unity from a common setting, a single narrator, a chrono-logical order, a repeated protagonist, and/or a group of characters. Others take place in varied locales, are told by a variety of narrators, jump around in time, and/or feature a variety of characters. In such cases, repeated motifs, common struggles, and/or thematic echoes may provide more subtle cohesion. Whatever the degree of coherence, the work ultimately remains discontinuous—sometimes even fragmented—making it an appropriate expression of our contemporary reality.

Though the short story sequence form may be expressive of our lives today, its antecedents stretch back to our earliest narratives, related orally as the sagas of heroic figures in what have become the epics of a variety of cultures. Frame tales and story cycles appear frequently before the short story flourished as a genre, but the form as we know it today was launched in the nineteenth century as writers gathered related stories into published volumes, often linked by a common narrator or region.

The short story sequence came into its own in the twentieth century with such works as James Joyce's *Dubliners*, Sherwood Anderson's *Winesburg, Ohio*, Jean Toomer's *Cane*, Hemingway's *In Our Time*, Steinbeck's *Pastures of Heaven*, and Eudora Welty's *The Golden Apples*. Since then, the growth of the form has been exponential, with con-temporary authors across the globe exploring a variety of narrative possibilities for configuring extended works made from stories. Recognizing that Evans's work resides solidly in this tradition, his readers should be more appreciative of the way he has chosen to relate the story of his protagonist, reflecting the power of the significant moment in each story as well as depicting their cumulative impact.

Whatever form a writer chooses, readers inevitably respond to an engaging plot, connect with characters undergoing meaningful struggles, visualize the details of setting, relish sharp imagery, and un-consciously engage with the narrative voice. Evans provides us with all these pleasures in his stories, bringing us home with his protagonist to understand some of the fundamental truths of human experience in our time.

Dr. Robert M. Luscher
University of Nebraska at Kearney

Green Seasons is available on Amazon.

Scott Evans holds a Master's in English from the University of California, Davis, and taught at the University of the Pacific, including fiction writing and a course titled "Crime, Punishment and Justice" that introduced students to criminology. He also taught at Louisiana State University in Baton Rouge, one of the settings in his "literary" mysteries. These thrillers follow a resourceful college instructor named Joseph Lawrence Conrad who, in Tragic Flaws, *is accused of a series of brutal crimes.* First Folio *picks up approximately three years later when Joe receives the handwritten plays of William Shakespeare—but the handwriting is not Shakespeare's. The third book,* Sylvia's Secrets, *explores the life of Sylvia Plath. Joe is beckoned to London to help a colleague determine whether or not Plath's death was suicide or murder. The fourth book in the series, titled* The Paris Papers, *find Joe Conrad in Paris, where he is approached by someone claiming to have Hemingway's lost first novel manuscript—worth a fortune. His novel* The Caribbean Prisoner, *a thriller set in the Virgin Islands and Florida, takes readers on a Hemingwayesque journey reminiscent of* The Sun Also Rises, *through the torturous emotional depths of Camus'* The Stranger, *and finishes with a grand finale that echoes* A Few Good Men. *www.scottevansauthor.com*